MW00627210

Ifá

The Ultimate Guide to a System of Divination and Religion of the Yoruba People

Your Free Gift (only available for a limited time)

Thanks for getting this book! If you want to learn more about various spirituality topics, then join Mari Silva's community and get a free guided meditation MP3 for awakening your third eye. This guided meditation mp3 is designed to open and strengthen ones third eye so you can experience a higher state of consciousness. Simply visit the link below the image to get started.

https://spiritualityspot.com/meditation

Table of Contents

Introduction

The rich, complex heritage of the Ifá religion has deep roots in the soil of West Africa, in the region known as Yorubaland. Encompassing the three modern states of Nigeria, Benin, and Togo, over 75 percent of Yorubaland is found in Nigeria. With a population numbering 55 million, most residents of Yorubaland are ethnic Yoruba people.

From the Yoruba, Ifá arose, giving birth to religious expressions in the New World. Born across the Atlantic with the enslaved people who built that world on behalf of European colonialism, Ifá is the root of Santeria, Candomblé, Sango Baptism, and Voudon.

Through these New World religions and other spiritual practices arising in the African diaspora, Ifá's cosmology and principle characteristics have been diffused worldwide. While their manifestation in these "spinoffs" is markedly different, the roots remain, ever leading back to the fruitful soil of Mother Africa.

Despite the best efforts of colonialists in Africa to impose the Christian religion, Ifá has not only survived but thrived. New World reflections of Ifá began to migrate north to the United States from countries like Cuba, Haiti, and Brazil, bringing a new interest in an ancient way of worship and life that resonates with the descendants of those taken from the shores of Africa.

At the heart of Ifá is divination, a mediating link between humanity and the spirit world. Drawing on the oral traditions of Odù Ifá and the oral transmission of folk tales and prose from Babalawo (meaning "father of the secrets" or "father of wisdom") to Babalawo through time, divination in Ifá relies on the interpretation of signs provided by the tools of divination. These are used to arrive at the Odù—or narrative from Odù Ifá—which will instruct followers seeking guidance. Interpreted by the Babalawo, divination provides practitioners of Ifá with a way to discern the guidance of the spirit world and the direction in which fate is taking them.

For adherents of Ifá, it is more than a religion. Ifá is a connection to the world of the spirits and their will for individual human life. The folk tales and prose carried by the hallowed Babalawo guide practitioners, serving to draw wisdom from the common scenarios of life for the conduct of their own lives. Ifá is founded on intellectual development—which leads to the perfection of individual lives—and the wisdom of the spirits shared with the living. In that development is the motivation for those who follow the Ifá religion—the soul's journey as an active, intentional consecration of human life to the will of the Divine.

In this book, you will discover a unique religion as old as 8,000 years. A religion that is still practiced to this day. The United Nations Educational Scientific and Cultural Association (UNESCO) named the religion a Masterpiece of Oral and Intangible Heritage of Humanity.

Explore Ifá, its divination practices, and spiritual disciplines. Enter a world guided by the hunger to transcend through ancient mysteries.

Chapter One: What Is Ifá?

"The song changes, so the drumming changes to suit it." — Yoruba Proverb

The proverb above is a good place to start our journey to the heart of Ifá. Ifá is more than a religion; Ifá is the command center of life. The faithful find meaning, direction, and the abiding comfort of spiritual guidance tethered to the intellect within its embrace.

This is one of Ifá's most striking features. While it is clear that the Near Eastern monotheistic faiths (Judaism, Christianity, and Islam) call on the intellect for those of the clerical class, the laity (those not ordained to the sacramental and/or pastoral service of God) are often called only to believe. The converse is true of Ifá, in which intellectual development is a component of the spirituality of the faithful.

The song in the quote is, of course, life. And, as we all know, the song of life has all kinds of changes. The drumming changes a lot as we move along on the journey. This is the true genius of Ifá. Human beings seeking guidance from the spirits through divination are connected in ritual. More than that, they are engaged intellectually, working with what they learn from the Divine Will.

In this first chapter, you will discover the history of Ifá and learn about the ethnic group it originated from, the Yoruba.

Who Are the Yoruba?

Until 1292 BCE, ancient Egypt was ruled by Nubian pharaohs. At this time—the nineteenth Dynasty—the rule of this ancient monarchy fell into the hands of Eurasian and Arabic monarchs (see the Resources section).

Taharqa, the Nubian Pharoah.

Migrating from what is now Saudi Arabia, the Biblical "Cushites" arrived in the Nile Valley to establish themselves there and to become a vital part of ancient Egypt, its culture, leadership, and religious expression. After thousands of years, these people were known as the "Yoruba."

The Yoruba worshipped a pantheon of deities as the Cushites of the Arabian Peninsula and brought their system of beliefs with them. As their influence grew as philosophical and spiritual leaders, those beliefs came to be part of the fabric of ancient Egypt's religious framework. In the sophistication and complexity of Egyptian beliefs, the echoes of the Cushites and a foretaste of Ifá can be readily observed.

The oral traditions of the Yoruba recount a migration from ancient Egypt—of which Nubia formed a part—bringing with them the ways of Egypt, refined from the earlier ways of Arabia. The monarchical system of the Yoruba bears a striking resemblance to that of ancient Egypt. However, burial practices and art also speak to this connection. Even today, many Yoruba trace their origins to Egypt and the Nile Valley. While there is much divergence on the part of archaeologists and historians, the Yoruba themselves adhere to this general version of events in establishing what became the Yoruba people in Yorubaland.

But until 1830, the word "Yoruba" was not used to describe these people. The term described a series of ethnic subgroups related by custom, regional origin, and religious practice. These were groups like the Oyo, Ketu, and Egba. The Yoruba were then living in city-states—which still characterize the political organization of today's Yorubaland.

Wandering through the ancient Near East, establishing in Egypt and then moving on again to Nigeria, Togo, and Benin, the Yoruba were dispersed by the Trans-Atlantic Slave Trade. Finally, they culminated in the Yoruba identity in Yorubaland as it is known today and brought a version of Ifá belief to the New World with the enslaved.

Ifá — The Touchstone of Yoruba Life

The word "Ifá" seems not to travel well, like many words in all languages. Boiled down as a central theme, it means an attraction, and in that attraction is the role Ifá plays in Yoruba life.

The attraction in question is to spiritual and material wisdom, simultaneously resulting in an improvement and purification of the practitioner's life. The human intellect is enlisted to work with the interpretations of the father priest, the Babalawo, or Iyalawo, the female priest, concerning divination (which will be discussed later). The result is a combination of lessons received in divination and how the practitioner lives those lessons in real-time.

The church of Ifá is the human being because it is in the human being that the wishes of the spirit world are realized. By learning from the wisdom of the spirits, Ifá practitioners are guided into a life radiant with both spiritual and practical meaning. There is no genuine division between the spirit and the body. In Ifá, they are one, just as the faithful are one with the spirit world through the divination expertise of the learned "father/mother priests."

All that is—living, dead, and yet to be, material and spiritual—is one. In this universal unity with the Divine source is the integrated philosophy of Ifá. It is a religion permeating every corner of the practitioner's life, just as the Divine infuses the Created Order with its numinous presence. There is no genuine division—save for cosmology (which will be discussed shortly). There is only unity. Each human participates in that unity as a planned component of the greater whole.

Ifá, then, is an attraction of the human soul to a Divine blueprint for living. In living as an integral part of a planned construct, the individual is not obligated to participate. Instead, Ifá calls counsel and steers the faithful in the right direction, hoping that the lessons stick. When they do not, an opportunity for more learning presents itself.

Governing all human behavior in Ifá are the Sixteen Commandments of the Faith.

Ifá's Sixteen Commandments (Ika Ofun)

Please note that you will see many versions of the Sixteen Commandments of Ifá online. The translation and personal interpretation play a part in the differences.

These commandments are the pillars of Ifá, fortifying the community with individual integrity that creates a microcosm of wholeness.

1. **Do Not Lie**

   Lying, in Ifá, is viewed as a failure of wisdom, intellect, and spirit. It is, therefore, a shortcoming that will eventually harm the life of the practitioner. The goal of Ifá is to eradicate the urge to lie and replace it with wise responses from lessons learned.

2. **Do Not Practice Ifá Without Understanding**

   Pay special attention to this commandment. Ifá is not a mud puddle for dabblers to splash in. It is an ancient and profound religion and way of life. No aspect of Ifá, including divination, should be approached without understanding and reverence.

3. **Do Not Mislead**

   To mislead is to tell untruths, so the commandment not to mislead addresses the practitioner's duty not to harm the community by steering any member of it in the wrong direction. The associated human cost can be very high.

4. **Do Not Cheat**

   Are you detecting a theme? Dishonesty is such a huge "no-no" in Ifá that three closely related variations are included in its major prescriptions for living. In this instance, cheating refers specifically to money and spirituality.

5. **Do Not Pretend to Be Wiser Than You Are**

   We all know someone who claims to have in-depth knowledge of various subjects but, in truth, knows only the headlines. Ifá directly forbids such vain posturing, counseling that wisdom is attained through the intellect and spirit working together and cannot be feigned.

6. **Be Humble**

Humility is woven into the fabric of Ifá in the meaning of the word. The attraction of the faithful is to wisdom, intellectual, and spiritual development. To attain these things, the humility of learning how to be a better human being teaches the commandment itself.

7. **Do Not Be Sneaky or Treacherous**

Sneakiness, betrayal, and manipulation are all hallmarks of disordered, unhappy people. Those who seek to manipulate others, and sneak around behind their backs to sow confusion and discontent, are not living sanctified lives but breaking lives for the ego's sake.

8. **Taboos and Superstition Have No Power Over You**

Here is where we encounter the practical orientation of Ifá. Taboos and superstitions are primarily cultural, leading to outlandish beliefs that have the power to knock the faithful off their course of sanctified communal living. They contribute nothing to life and should have no influence.

9. **Do Not be Arrogant About Taboos and Superstitions**

Western societies have plenty of cultural taboos and superstitions. Many of us tend to laugh at them. Ifá prohibits this, and the commandment to be humble precludes any derisive display in their confrontation. Rather, any belief in their power is met with studied neutrality.

10. **Be Trustworthy**

Being someone that other people can consistently trust is the hallmark of a well-developed person. Having learned the wisdom of the spirits and ancestors, the Ifá adherent does not tell others' secrets and keeps promises.

11. **Respect the Challenges of Others**

Expressed as the command to not take the cane from the hand of a blind person, this commandment counsels the active support of those with challenges like blindness, mobility issues, deafness, muteness, or any other challenge that makes them vulnerable to the ill will of others. These people are not to be interfered with but supported. All challenges of any kind are viewed as an opportunity to model decency.

12. Respect Your Elders

Near the end of their earthly journeys, older people are unquestioningly respected as those who have gathered wisdom and lessons from Ifá. They are living wisdom and, thus, sacred exemplars.

13. Respect Other People's Marriages/Relationships

Sexual morality means not interfering with the relationships and marriages of others by setting your sights on one of the partners. It also means being sincere with your sexual partners and not misrepresenting yourself.

14. Do Not Sexually Betray a Friend

Of all the marriages and relationships Ifá practitioners should not mess with, their friends' are at the top of the list. Sexually engaging with a friend's wife or husband represents a profound rupture in the integrity of the community.

15. Do Not Betray Secrets

Disseminating information entrusted to you destroys your community standing and the ability of other people to trust you. It provokes cynicism and social isolation.

16. Do Not Disrespect the Priests

The priests of Ifá are in place to guide the community with their knowledge gained from years of training. To disrespect the priests is to disrespect the deposit of oral history and tradition they have been entrusted with and, by extension, to disrespect Ifá itself.

The Role of Divination

Divination is a central ritual focus in Ifá, used to provide the faithful with guidance and growth. This book is largely concerned with this aspect of the Faith, but it is helpful to know what divination is intended to achieve.

Divination's centrality to believers' governance and philosophical framework is its communal strength. It is used for everything from discerning the will of the spirit world for a new year to selecting a new leader, and divination also serves the faithful as a means of both following and shifting their destiny.

Because in Ifá, destiny is written by the Divine, but it's also "plastic." Its malleability is in the willingness of the individual practitioner to take control of what life has in store to change fortune's trajectory. Divination takes the temperature of existing worldly conditions, consults with spirit, and prescribes remedial action. Divination also serves the faithful by reminding them that spirit is in control of all that is and that only through intercession can human beings protect themselves from the vagaries of an uncertain world.

For big and small questions, divination is not a passive process to attract good fortune and protect against bad fortune. The agency of the person approaching the Babalawo/Iyalawo for a reading starts the process. While divination provides answers, it's entirely up to the person seeking the spirit world's guidance to act on those answers. Divination is of little use to the person seeking it without this implied and expected participation.

However, there is a more serious consequence involved when the guidance of divination is not acted upon.

In Heaven, as It Is on Earth

As seen in the Sixteen Commandments of Ifá, this religion and lifestyle are rooted in common decency: Respect for other people, humility, and self-awareness. These qualities describe humanity on its best behavior.

The emphasis on orthopraxy—right action, as opposed to "orthodoxy" or right thinking—points to a functional reason for that emphasis. Simply, what happens on earth does not stay on earth. Rather, what happens on earth has repercussions in the spirit world (heaven).

Thus, for the sake of the integrity of the spirit world, entangled with the material world through the Divine spirit that lives far away in the heavens, divination stands in the gap. The gap, of course, is that of the flesh and its errant ways. Divination teaches the flesh the ways of spirit by divining its wisdom through the agency of priestly expertise and the tools used (which will be discussed later).

When human beings in the community adhere to the perfection of their spirits, they hold up to heaven. This is not only for heaven's sake but also for their own. The world of the spirits is the promise of life's other side, hidden deep within us as our portion. That portion is not genuinely ours. It is a gift of the Divine, not unlike a ticket to the ultimate rave. While through the soul, we are fully integrated with all that is, our flesh must convey us through life's lessons. While the flesh is created and holy, it is also the site of our most damaging human traits. The flesh is where we learn and what we purify in that learning toward the perfection of the spirit.

Divination's central role in Ifá reveals a fundamental truth about this spiritual lifestyle. The unity of all things is impacted by humanity's willingness to examine itself and to seek out the spirit in that examination. In divination, Ifá adds a functional learning tool that feeds the spirit as lessons are absorbed in the flesh. When the flesh is no longer at war with spirit, it has evolved to model more of its potential—but there is an eternity for human potential to develop fully, in Ifá.

The Sixteen Commandments are clear. They proscribe the communally corrosive and prescribe the socially constructive. In demanding individual fidelity to a common standard of virtuous conduct, the Commandments reinforce the integrity of spirit, knitting the Created Order into union with its Divine source. When the good on earth is multiplied, the integrity of heaven is fortified. This unity, in Ifá, is expressed in communal fidelity, which mirrors divinely mandated unity between the Created and the Creator.

Wisdom and Intellect

Ifá is loosely translated as "attraction." That attraction is to the pursuit of wisdom sparked by intellect and touched by the spirit. But wisdom and intellect are not for their own sake in Ifá. They serve a much larger purpose.

That purpose is the ordering of the universe through the orthopraxy of righteous people. This righteousness is not for its own sake, either. Rather, it serves the greater goal, which is the unity and integrity of all. It reserves the resolution of the errant, egotistical ways of the flesh, directing the individual toward the way that serves the community and, thus, the goal.

In Ifá, wisdom and intellect have a divine source, and that is OlOdù mare, the creator deity of Ifá and the source of the Created Order.

In the next chapter, you will meet OlOdù mare, find out about the origin of Ifá divination, and discover the Ifá version of the Creation narrative.

Chapter Two: God and the Great High Priest

OlOdù mare, the name of God in Ifá, has a very familiar profile. To start with, OlOdù mare (also known as Olorun) is called the Lord of Heaven and Creator. Like the God of the Hebrew and Christian Scriptures, OlOdù mare is not a creature but so completely "Other" and ontologically inscrutable that human beings cannot even begin to conceive Their substance.

OlOdù mare is sometimes described as the "Monarch who can't be found, even if you search earnestly." This ineffability and otherness align with the God of the Hebrew Scriptures. They, when quizzed by Moses as to Their name, replied, "I am what I am" (expressed in Hebrew as "YHVH," the Tetragrammaton, Exodus 3:14). This ineffability is similarly emphasized in Ifá's conceptualization of the Divine.

OlOdù mare's story is of a god removed. Once near the Creation wrought by his hand, the God of Ifá became remote yet accessible. Ever near in spirit to Creation, OlOdù mare continued to connect with people and hear their pleas. The similarities—superficially—end between the God of Ifá and the God of the Hebrew and Christian Scriptures. Because, while reachable, OlOdù mare knew they needed an emissary on the ground.

The Ifá Creation Narrative

Long, long ago, Olodumare lived nearer to humanity's home than he does now. There was no question that we were within each other's reach. God was one of us—a neighbor just down the block.

However, then, humanity got arrogant. Humanity began to plunder heaven indiscriminately and disrespectfully, raiding the food of the heavenly precincts and throwing apple cores on the ground. Olodumare was not amused.

Thus, our "neighbor just down the block" packed up and moved further away from us, worn out from yelling, "Get off my lawn!" We know where Olodumare lives and vice versa, but we take each other in small doses, still smarting from that long-ago squabble that came between us.

Before that happened, many interchanges occurred between Olodumare in heaven above and humanity on earth below. This is depicted in Ifá as a swampy wasteland (as in the Biblical Creation narrative where the earth is described as "formless and void" Genesis 1: 2). Thanks to a chain that connected heaven and earth, this interchange occurred, allowing two-way free passage.

Olodumare is in heaven and humanity below.
https://unsplash.com/photos/Fem4uCQ7VEg

Olodumare saw the earth's state, so he instructed Obatala (Ifá's co-creative Orisha, see Chapter Three) to clean it up and make it solid. OlOdù mare gave Obatala the tools to follow his instructions: A snail shell filled with dirt, a pigeon, and a hen.

So, Obatala set off, and when he arrived at the swampy mess the earth was, he threw the dirt from the snail shell and let the pigeon and hen fly off to spread it around. Obatala then commanded a chimera to check on the work of the birds and pronounce its sound.

The chimera reported that the earth still needed more work as parts of it were not yet up to snuff. The chimera then returned for a second inspection, after which he reported to Obatala that the work had been completed.

Obatala returned to OlOdù mare's presence and reported success. OlOdù mare then gave Obatala another commission—equipping the earth with all needed to sustain life. Obatala, deciding this was a big job, took Orunmila (the oracle Orisha) with him as an advisor.

First, the palm tree was created to give food, oil, leaves to build homes with, and the fruit's juice to drink. Then, Obatala received three more fruit-bearing trees for humans to derive juice from, as there was no rain yet. The hen and the pigeon would become the ancestors of all birds.

Olodumare asked Obatala to take sixteen humans he had created in the heavenly precincts to the earth when all this work was completed. Obatala was then instructed to create forms in human shape, as Obatala could not give them life. As the God of Ifá, only Olodumare could give life to the forms. Thus, he did, breathing into their nostrils to animate them. (NB: Another remarkable similarity to the Genesis Creation narrative, see Genesis 2: 7.)

The Origin of Divination

Olodumare asked Orunmila to remain on the earth to counsel the faithful through the medium of divination. As mentioned, divination may be employed to arrive at communal decisions about leadership. For individual practitioners, though, it serves as a touchstone, providing supplicants with valuable information and empowering them to change their lives and destinies by using their intellects and spirits in unison.

In recent times, divination has joined forces with our material world's scientific and intellectual institutions, with the spirits counseling practitioners to seek the help of doctors, lawyers, and other professionals. However, divination stands as a message of OlOdù mare's love for humanity. It provides a means by which the living can seek the counsel of the spirit world, deriving better lives and living more happily and fruitfully in the process.

Divination is a spiritual tool that serves the faithful and the community they live in, dispensing advice, giving answers to questions, and these days, directing them to help professionals to accomplish the leading of the spirit.

Because OlOdù mare moved away from the earth, Orunmila acts as his intermediary, replacing the in situ Divine Presence with that of a proxy, overseeing the conduct of divination and the fitness and expertise of those charged with sharing its gifts, the Babalawo/Iyalawo. It was also Orunmila who established the Ifá's oral tradition, the Odù Ifá. For this, he is known as the High Priest and Revelator of OlOdù mare's divinity and the prophetic gift of divination. (NB: For this purpose, the Biblical interpretation of prophecy is to "reveal." Specifically, prophecy reveals truths that liberate.)

And because divination sprang from the mind of the Creator, OlOdù mare, divination is a sacred center of life for those who practice Ifá. Complex in its practice and a sacred link between the people and their God, divination is that chain between heaven and earth whose links by the Oracle, Orunmila, are strengthened with each lesson learned and acted on.

The Distant God

The retraction of OlOdù mare from the earth is, in truth, the very heart of the need for divination in the Divine mind. Human beings were rude, vulgar, and obnoxious. They needed their Creator, but there is only so much a loving god can handle. OlOdù mare solved the problem of Their anger by moving far enough away from human beings to reduce the temptation to punish them.

Instead, God left an emissary on earth to sort things out. Humanity looked fine, but it was not. The situation demanded a prolonged tweak to set it straight—and that tweak was divination. Through divination, the community of Ifá is ordered toward greater fidelity with the original prototype of humanity. With the support of the learned Babalawo/Iyalawo, divination turned the community's mind to self-development in the service of the Divine-human relationship, weaving it carefully back together in respectful service to something greater than the self.

OlOdù mare is distant from humanity in cosmology but near in the person of Orunmila and the gift of divination. Through Orunmila, the Almighty acts to repair a damaged humanity, void of respect for its Creator and heaven itself. Returning to the Sixteen Commandments of Ifá in Chapter One, we can see that the Ifá Creation story is the reason for Ifá's appeal to honesty, orthopraxy, and humility.

Restoring the Connection

The world's religions and their Creation narratives usually point to a rupture of some sort at the time or immediately after the time of Creation. The Hebrew Scriptures tell the story of Eve's consumption of an apple as that rupture. The Kabbalah of the Jewish Mystical tradition offers a complex, technical description of a layered Creation of four worlds with a fifth near the seat of the Divine. This is the world of primordial man, Adam Kadmon—the spiritual prototype of the Adam of the Garden, near God's heart, yet unrealized in the Garden version.

The two Adams and God's fractured relationship with the physical representation of Adam, the primordial man, holds out Adam Kadmon as the exemplar of Divine intent. With OlOdù mare, divination provides the curative solution to the rupture. In traditional Judaism, the 613 mitzvot (commandments) perform similarly, restoring the Divine-human relationship.

The Commandments of Ifá work hand in hand with divination to build the type of human OlOdù mare intended to place on the earth—honest, humble, and just of action. Throughout life, the quest of Ifá's faithful is to become more just, humble, and honest, thus saving the original wound with obeisance to the work of the Creator God.

A restored connection between OlOdù mare and the people of Ifá is a restored Creation, healed by the loving connections of community and the connection of that community to a distant God. With the advice and learning provided by divination, the work of Ifá becomes an education for graceful, peaceful living. That process is one of healing shared between God and humanity.

One Creator God

OlOdù mare, despite the many names by which They are called, is only one God, situated as the source of all that is and the reason for all things, visible or invisible. In the next chapter, you will learn more about the Orisha, but they're often held up as evidence of a pantheistic model, which is not true of Ifá. Ifá is a monotheistic religion, just as Christianity, Judaism, and Islam are.

In the world of Ifá, all live in God's world and God, as all is within the context of the Supreme Being. There is no Church building. There is no hierarchy. There are roles fulfilled by people chosen to fulfill them, and the Orisha ordained by OlOdù mare to act as guides and helpers to humanity. Orunmila and Obatala are both Orisha, fulfilling specific roles, as directed by OlOdù mare. It is important to note that Orisha's spiritual beings were created by OlOdù mare, like everything and everyone else.

While it is futile to compare the roles of the Orisha, who are spiritual beings, to those of Angels or Saints, perhaps it's helpful to think of them as aspects of God, sent to work on behalf of the same distant Deity. This will be explored in more depth in Chapter Three, but it's helpful to have an idea as we talk more about divination from the perspective of God's relationship with humanity. It's important to understand that we are discussing a monotheistic Faith. To do that, we need to understand that the Orisha are not "gods" but rather facilitators of God and, like Obatala (High Priest) and Orunmila (Oracle), emissaries.

Another factor compelling some to depict Ifá as a polytheistic Faith is its sitting in Africa. It is not unusual for the West to mischaracterize African Faiths in this way. Colonialism brought with it the Christian Faith, and part of the colonialist project was to impose that Faith without compromise. There is also the matter of the many names of OlOdù mare.

This second reason for the polytheistic fallacy concerning Ifá is strange, as the God of the Hebrew Scriptures also has many names, from El-Shaddai to YHVH to Elohim. Thus, it is important to understand that this is a Western interpretation rooted in the usual human demand for priority in all things and a general lack of respect for practices and beliefs not native to them. That human demand is at the heart of the colonialist imposition of Christianity on populations who already had religious beliefs.

OlOdù mare is the most common name in Ifá for the Creator God, but regional variations have occurred with the diffusion of faiths to other regions and parts of the world. As we are discussing the traditional ways of Yoruba, here are the names OlOdù mare is known by in those communities of Faith:

- Oriki Edumare
- Oriki OlOdù mare
- Oriki Olorun
- Oriki Oluwa
- Oriki Odùmare

How we choose to name God is none of our business—as the narrative in the Book of Exodus discussed earlier so poignantly makes clear. The names of God exist to comfort the people by giving God a name that might be spoken in supplication. However, what is Divine can never be definitively named any more than it might be definitively known or described, despite humanity's most Herculean efforts.

The Attributes of Olodumare

The attributes of Olodumare are largely parallel to those of God in the three Monotheistic Faiths. As Creator, Olodumare is also all-knowing, all-powerful, the judge of all, without beginning or end, and the site of holiness.

Those attributes have uniqueness, reality, control, and complete, inviolable unity. Olodumare is reality itself in which all that exists resides, yet transcending the material and created. God, in this model, exists for Themselves in greatness as the immaterial First Cause, ultimate mystery, and eternality itself. From

---

Olodumare flow fidelity, love, mercy, kindness, and all that is pure and good.

These attributes will sound familiar to practitioners of Islam, Christianity, and Judaism as the attributes of God described in their sacred books and practice. This familiarity brings us back to the journey of the Yoruba people to Nigeria.

From the Arabian Peninsula and its sacred cities, Mecca and Medina, the Yoruba cut across what is today known as the Middle East to arrive in Egypt. Who did they meet on that journey? Who did they absorb the cultural practices of? Who did they exchange their own cultural practices with?

The common threads running through Ifá, Judaism, Christianity, and Islam concerning the nature of God and the Creation narrative tell us a fascinating, ancient story. The bubbling cauldron of the ancient Near East contains myriad mysteries. The migratory trajectory of the Yoruba hints at some of them.

But when you are discussing an 8,000-year-old religion—senior to even the first of Near Eastern Monotheistic Faiths, Judaism—existing in a volatile, ancient world, the threads of history can become tangled. Any religion related to the ancient Near East is bound to have picked up and left behind various impressions and expressions as part of its journey through time and such religiously rich territories.

The Distant God Is Not Worshipped

Although Ifá is a monotheistic Faith, OlOdù mare is not expressly worshiped in Ifá. Rather, worship is directed to the emissaries of the distant God in the Orisha. Removed from humanity, OlOdù mare's presence is realized through the created spiritual beings representing Them and the ritual frameworks established for that purpose, especially divination.

The next chapter discusses Orisha and their counterparts, the Ajogun. Through the Orisha, humanity rediscovers its intended state. It returns to OlOdù mare's intention of creating it by communing with the Orisha through the agency of the Babalawo/Iyalawo.

Chapter Three: Emissaries and Stumbling Blocks

In the Ifá religion, as with its New World offshoots (Santeria, Voudon, et al.), Orisha stands as humanity's link to the Divine Reason at the center of the universe. Having moved out of range, OlOdù mare makes Their presence known through the Orisha, standing as representatives, emissaries, living links, and counselors interceding in human affairs on their behalf.

However, in the cosmology of Ifá, the world has a shadow side expressed in the presence of the Ajogun. While the Orisha are emissaries and helpers, the Ajogun are the stumbling blocks of the cosmos, leading humanity astray with ill intention.

Let us find out more about these two sides of Ifá's cosmological setup and what they mean in the context of religion, starting with the sunny side.

Mileage May Vary – The Orisha

Ifá lore insists that there are so many Orisha that they cannot be counted. At the same time, it is generally agreed that there are 400 of them, plus one. What this means is not that there are, in reality, 401 Orisha; it means that 400 plus one is an expression of limitless in the context of Ifá. The truth is that Orisha encompasses a wide variety of spiritual entities, including nature spirits who may be regionally appealed to but are otherwise unknown in the greater context of Ifá. Shortly, we shall talk about some of the Orisha known as the Seven African Powers, but it's important to remember that Ifá tradition itself numbers the Orisha variously. Depending on the specific community's oral tradition and source, it may be 400 or 1,400. The point is that the Orisha are numerous, and because they represent OlOdù mare, the mystery is entirely in order.

As pointed out, there is little illumination to be had in comparing the spiritual entities of Ifá with those of other faith systems. They are who they are, and the grace knows them through the religious system of which they form a vital part.

The most compelling description of the Orisha is that of emissaries of the Divine attributes and will. However, most of the Orisha were once like us—human beings. Having passed over to the spirit world, their destiny was to serve OlOdù mare as his emissaries and ordering agents. When you consider the immensity of such a commission and its Holy Source, it is a small wonder that there is no definitive number when it comes to the Orisha.

The Ajogun

Every cosmology needs balance. Without darkness, how is light distinguishable? Without evil, how is good known and defined? Ifá is no exception to this rule, with the balancing agent expressed as the Ajogun.

The problem of evil in Ifá is explained by the Eight Ajogun, who sow disease, discord, strife, misery, death, and chaos in human life. When they present themselves, the community's help to repel them is sought with the support of the learned Babalawo/Iyalawo.

We all know that everything in this world is not, by any means, good. The Judeo-Christian tradition explains this deficit in Creation with the fall of humanity in the Garden of Eden. In Ifá, evil in Creation is explained by these rogue spirits.

Unlike the Orisha, the Ajogun is not of human origin. They were never like us. Rather they express the negative aspects of the natural world and the adversity faced in every human life.

Before we meet some of these emissaries and stumbling blocks, let us talk about an unusual presence in the cosmology of Ifá—that of Eshu, the Divine Messenger and spirit of the crossroads.

OlOdù mare's Divine Messenger

One of Ifá's Orisha present at Creation, and thus, primordial, Eshu is the ordering agent mediating between life and death at the crossroads. Known for mischievousness, death, misfortune, and trickery, Eshu holds a special place in the cosmology of Ifá. Ensuring order and balance, Eshu is the communications director between humanity and OlOdù mare and the gatekeeper of communications with Orisha.

The Divine Messenger is also in charge of conveying sacrifices to the heavenly precincts to the Orisha they are intended for. But as Eshu is charged with balance, he also distributes sacrificial offerings to the Ajogun.

One of Eshu's primary traits is that he can go between good and evil. For this reason, he is sometimes cast as both Orisha and Ajogun. However, the truth is that he's neither, definitively. Eshu represents the continuing balance in Creation, dispensing the extremes of human existence according to his whim. He's as unpredictable as human life, reminding practitioners that "bad things happen to good people."

Because of this unpredictability, Eshu is known by more than 200 names, speaking to the diversity of action he's responsible for. Sometimes known as an "avenger" of wrongdoing, Eshu is also known to compel evildoing in humans for unknown purposes. Eshu presides over death and punishes the wicked, standing at the crossroads as God's gatekeeper and guiding the dead into life's next chapter.

Now that you have an idea of Ifá's cosmology, let us look at some of the major characters in that cosmology, starting with Orisha.

Major Orisha to Know

As this book is intended to introduce Ifá divination, it will limit it to the Seven African Powers. These are the principal Orisha of Ifá and are reasonably consistent in Ifá communities wherever they are found.

The Seven African Powers are also present in New World offshoots of Ifá, like Voudon, Candomble, and Santeria. These seven are the most powerful and evocative and, thus, the most widely revered of all the Orisha:

1. Orunmila
2. Obatala
3. Oshun
4. Ogun
5. Yemaya
6. Shango
7. Elegua

Of these seven, Shango is revered as the "king" of the Orisha, a powerful and fearsome Orisha charged with the stewardship and deployment of thunder. As with all that is concerned with unraveling the complexity of this ancient religion, the Seven African Powers may appear differently in different settings—for example, in Cuba, Babalu-Aye may be included in the place of one of the seven listed above.

There is some debate about the status of these seven Orisha, most of it centering on the presumed syncretism Ifá experienced under colonialism. But as with Santeria in Cuba, the Catholic Church was only appeased by Ifá practitioners. The Saints of the Church were superimposed, never obscuring the original identity of the Orisha masked by colonialism's wishful thinking. The Seven African Powers are not, as some suggest, Catholic Saints who are "not Orisha." Rather, they are Orisha who were hidden from the Church using its own iconography and thus preserved in their original, un-colonized form.

1. **Orunmila**

   In the Ifá Creation narrative, we met Orunmila, charged with being the link to OlOdù mare through divination. Through Orunmila, humanity is given the gift of spirituality and communication with the Divine and access to the Divine plan for their lives.

   Orunmila is the Orisha of wisdom and prophecy, moving among humanity as its spiritual advisor. He is also a co-creator, along with Obatala.

2. **Obatala**

   Again, we have met Obatala in the Creation story. Obatala acted as the "hands" of OlOdù mare in creating the universe. Obatala is the primordial Orisha, known in Ifá as humanity's co-creator and original sculptor. As you will recall, Obatala fashioned the human form, but OlOdù mare breathed life into it. The Yoruba say that he continues to form humans in the womb.

3. **Oshun**

   This female Orisha presides over Creation's rivers. She represents the font of Divine love, fertility, human love and romance, and the sweetness of life. She is both revered for her gentleness and feared for her temper. As mercurial and double-edged as water itself, Oshun's love can turn to rage when she is not respected.

4. **Ogun**

   Presiding over metal and manipulating metals through alchemy, Ogun is believed to be made of iron himself. Ogun's sector is healing, but this Orisha is also sometimes compelled to destroy. Strength is Ogun's vibration, with a special place in his spiritual realm for families. Children, especially, are protected by Ogun.

5. **Yemaya**

   Another female Orisha, Yemaya, is charged with water stewardship, like Oshun. But where Oshun's reign is over rivers, Yemaya's is over oceans. She protects women, children, and those who take to the ocean to fish and travel. Like Oshun and water itself, Yemaya can be unpredictable. However, she saves her tenderest care for abused women crying out for help and safety.

6. Shango

The Orisha of thunder, Shango, is intensely masculine. Dispensing justice with the lightning and thunder he commands, Shango is the archetypal male protector and hero. He is also virile, availing himself of female Orisha for his pleasure. He is revered as an ancient King of the Yoruba, becoming an Orisha after death. Once living as one of the most powerful leaders in human form, he's considered an Orisha of fearsome potency.

7. Elegua (Eshu)

Finally, we have Elegua (Eshu, the Divine Messenger). While unique among the Orisha and not strictly one of them (see OlOdù mare's Divine Messenger, earlier in this chapter), he stands as one of the Seven African Powers. Presiding over the crossroads where life and death converge, Elegua is a trickster and the official Guide to the Precincts of the Afterlife. This communications director allows humanity contact with the Orisha and, by extension, OlOdù mare.

Without Evil, What Is Goodness?

As with any other religious system, Ifá makes accommodation for the problem of evil. In the Hebrew Scriptures, the Book of Job dispatches this problem by explaining why bad things happen to good people.

Ifá's strategy concerning the problem of evil is not unlike that of modern ultra-Orthodox Judaism—devotion, prayer, and ritual. And as the Haredim of Judaism believe, the integration of religious belief into daily life is fundamental. The 613 mitzvot are a constant reminder of spiritual duty, and the Sixteen Commandments and 263 Odùs accomplish the same in Ifá.

Ifa's approach to good and evil quite similar to that of Judaism.

Yoruba cosmology sees Creation as a gourd cut in half. Because of humanity's offensive behavior in the heavenly precincts, compelling OlOdù mare to move off the block, we live in one half alone. OlOdù mare and the Orisha (and ancestors) live in a far-removed "heavenly" half of Creation. Between these two halves reside the Ajogun and other evil spirits.

Without the orthopraxy (right action), ritual devotion, and prayerful worship of Ifá devotees, the Ajogun would wreak havoc, throwing Creation out of whack and creating chaos. As with the Haredim of Judaism, followers of Ifá believe that consecrating their daily lives to God keeps Creation from spinning out of control with the incursion of evil.

A constant in the cosmology of Ifá is death itself, framed as an inevitable part of human life and inseparable from it. For the Yoruba, death is inevitable, indivisible but not the end of anything.

Death is, in fact, a gateway to another chapter of life in the other half of the gourd. However, there are different values attached to death depending on when it arrives in the deceased person's life. For example, the elderly dying is greeted with jubilation. This is not because the old has died but because they have lived out their earthly quest for holiness. In the case of children or babies dying, the community reacts with sadness. That sadness has little to do with age, except in the reality that early death deprives the soul of life's journey toward holiness and sanctification. Death due to an accident or human interference (murder) is viewed similarly.

But the death of children is sometimes attributed to the principle of "abiku," in which children are reincarnated and never destined to reach adulthood. This is seen as a perpetual denial of the spirit's ascension and, thus, a curse. Abiku is translated as "spirit children" (children who have been denied the fullness of their spiritual potential).

The cosmology of Ifá recognizes no "final judgment." Rather, the lives we live stand as our testaments, typified by either vice or virtue. The community remembers us for what we have done in life, indicating the truth of our spiritual journeys on earth and our lessons. How we behave is how we proceed to the next chapter.

Without evil, there is no goodness. We cannot understand what is deemed "good" without the benchmark of evil providing a juxtaposition. And so, the cosmology of Ifá is intimately tied to the problem of evil and humanity's crucial role in containing it. With the Ajogun representing natural evil, a kind of contamination of Creation, the Divine OlOdù mare is separated from us. This immaterial wall of evil separates the two halves of the gourd. Ifá teaches worthy living, just action, and intense devotion to manage that wall's presence.

The next chapter explores the tools of Ifá. These are the physical components of divination as handed down at Creation and developed by the hands of humanity through the counsel of Orunmila. Let us see how the Babalawo/Iyalawo works with these tools to guide and counsel their communities and draw them forward on their spiritual journeys.

Chapter Four: The Tools of Ifá

This book explores an 8,000-year-old religion, Ifá, which is complex and not to be trifled with. If you are attracted to Ifá, we pray that your journey is blessed. However, even if that is the case, Ifá requires an intense initiation involving several stages and a complex set of ceremonies. Some of these ceremonies are private and secret to the practitioners of the religion. Even if you choose to be initiated into Ifá, you will not be using the tools described in this chapter. They are expressly reserved for the use of the Babalawo/Iyalawo, who has studied and trained for many years to ascend to the status of a learned spiritual teacher and guide.

In this era of instant gratification, our intention is not to proselytize but to inform, not to give license to dabblers but to share knowledge for the sake of interest. Thank you for respecting the practices of this ancient religion and its imperatives concerning membership and leadership.

The foundation of divination is the Odù—the verse that the Babalawo/Iyalawo is guided to by the casting done in divination. Divination leads to the revelation of the Odù as an answer to the supplicant's question, a solution to the challenge they are seeking divination to address.

The Babalawo/Iyalawo

The learned priest is the heart of Ifá, building on the communicative bridge represented by Orunmila, the spirit of wisdom. Orunmila, in turn, communicates all to OlOdù mare as the spiritual communications link between humanity and the Divine. The role of the priest is only attainable after a lengthy period of training and initiation—fifteen years by some accounts.

The priest is the "Father/Mother of Mysteries," divining the will of God in the lives of those he or she counsels. The "Ori" or "head" is the subject of the priest's work, which serves the individual destinies of community members and calls on them to apply intuition and intellect to life's challenges and questions.

Ori is the Divine spark in humanity. For this reason, it stands as an analog to the Orisha in the human body. Thus, while the Yoruba say that OlOdù mare has breathed life into them, the spark of that life is in the Divine attributes represented by the Orisha. Because of OlOdù mare's separation from humanity, the Divine spark's status is not directly Divine but mediated by Their attributes in Creation.

While Ifá priests are not necessarily selected for the vocation in childhood, children's spiritual gifts indicate "priest material." The prophetic role of the priest in divination is that of "clear sight," connecting the Ori of the person seeking counsel to Divine will and the power of the Orisha through the spirit of wisdom, Orunmila.

Orunmila may even be thought of as the first of all the priests. Having given human beings the gift of divination to ascertain the Divine will for their lives, he stands as the first in a long line of learned teachers, prophets, and counselors.

The role of the Babalawo/Iyalawo, while not limited to divination, is primarily that of a community resource, sharing the gift of Orunmila with the faithful. He is a shaman who seeks peace with all humanity, not just with the practitioners of Ifá. His commission is not only to those who share his beliefs but to humanity as a whole. A shaman, a traditional medicine man, and a healer of souls and bodies, the Babalawo/Iyalawo is the center of religious life in Ifá and the living link to the past, the future, and the heavenly realm of the spirits.

In divination, the Babalawo influences the status of problems or challenges in the lives of community members, calling on the intervention of Orunmila and other Orisha concerned with the person in question or the specific problem. The Babalawo has the power to influence outcomes by calling on this intervention, changing outcomes to those more favorable to the community member.

Women Priests — Tradition, Not Innovation

In most spiritual/religious traditions, women have been marginalized to the laity (those not ordained to serve the community). Despite indications in the scriptural record of religions like Christianity, where women fulfilled roles of ordained service in the earliest layer of the tradition, this is the universal truth.

Women played an important role as priestesses.
https://unsplash.com/photos/xZgkFQ4Hijc

For example, it was the "deaconess Phoebe" (Romans 1: 2) who bore the letter to the Romans—later to become a book in the Christian Scriptures—to the community in Rome. As she bore the letter, it would have been Phoebe who stood before that religious community to read its contents, written by Paul. While this latter function of the deaconess of the first century is assumed, the deacon's clerical role includes transmitting important information to the community from the bishop. Paul was not a bishop, as these did not exist at the time, but the modern deacon carries episcopal messages and delivers them to the parishes of any given diocese.

Primarily for reasons of social prohibition in Rome—women were relegated to a position lower than that of enslaved people)—women were marginalized out of leadership roles in the later Church, ceding these to men. It was not until the twentieth century that women began to regain their roles as leaders in sacramental worship and service to their communities.

However, the story of women's leadership in Ifá is very different. It is written right into the oral traditions of the religion, in the person of Orunmila's daughter. The story goes that Orunmila was asked why he was not initiating his daughter, Alara, into Ifá. He responded that she could not be because of her sex. He was corrected and advised that women had as much right to study Ifá as men. From then on, women were initiated into the priesthood.

IyanIfá and Iyalawo

While these two terms to describe women priests are used to define all women priests—especially online—there are some differences between the two.

"IyanIfá" is the more commonly used term, indicating stewardship of Ifá knowledge and the cultic empowerment required to engage in divination. "Iyalawo" is the more powerful of the two in terms of meaning.

"Iyalawo" indicates a person who has been graced with discernible spiritual gifts, traceable to the Creator God, OlOdù mare, through the wife of Orunmila, Odù—rumored by some branches of the Faith to have shared divination with Orunmila. Odù is considered the source of Aché (the spirit of humanity turned toward God and the life force). She is the primordial Iyalawo. In this last interpretation is the profound call to women in Ifá to take up the mantle of the priesthood.

Now, let us look at divination tools, what they are, how they're used, and their significance.

Opele — The Divining Chain

Viewed as the assistant of Orunmila, the divining chain echoes the form of the chain by which the Orisha (including Orunmila) traveled to the earthly realm from heaven. In its divining function, the Opele fulfills the same purpose figuratively, as a link between the two halves of Ifá's cosmological gourd.

Used primarily for minor divination work—daily concerns like money, sex, work, family, and romantic relationships or disputes between neighbors—the Opele is the most commonly used of all divination tools.

It is used by the Aseda and the Babalawo/Iyalawo, who might be likened to the deacon in the Christian clerical hierarchy, attending to the daily needs of the spiritual community, as opposed to the sacramental needs fulfilled by the priests.

The Opele consists of eight nuts of the Opele tree, divided in half and strung at equal intervals on a chain.

The chain is held at the center and swung gently. It is then laid out on a cloth in front of the priest. In a single motion, the priest creates a pattern, interpreted to correspond with an Odù (verse) of the oral tradition of Ifá, which is then recited.

Divination with Opele is part of a lifestyle in which the community is realigned with the Creator by taking their lives into their own hands by seeking the priest's counsel in divination. Ifá is considered primordial in the Faith and the general spiritual state of humanity as well. In the divination chain, practitioners find the solutions to their problems, solving them with the advice of Orunmila through the priest.

Ikin (Kola Nuts)

Ikin is nuts from the tropical Kola tree, called "Obi" or "Obi Abata" in the Yoruba language. The Obi Obata variety of Kola nut is sacred to Ifá. This type of nut from the Kola family consists of four lobes, which are the ones used in divination. The four-lobed Obi is also known as "Iya Obi" or "Mother Obi."

Kola Nuts.

The four-lobed Obi is used in divination due to the perception of balance between male and female energies, with two lobes representing the male sex and two the female sex. The number four represents stability and consistency inherent in the balance of energies.

Only when the Obi is split open are the four lobes revealed. They are distinguishable as male or female by the markings that appear down the center of the lobe. A single line terminating in a point indicates the sex for the male. For the female, the line splits in two, resulting in the shape of a "y."

The metaphysics of the Ifá religion specifies that all energies are divisible into male and female, but the distinction is not only concerned with the specificities of sex. The male/female dichotomy of energetic reality in Ifá provides a benchmark for understanding energy as a spiritual simulation of dichotomous mammalian sex.

All the usual attributes associated with the two sexes are present in the energetic interpretations of Ifá, without assigning them a value according to the sex they describe. While male energy is routinely typified as expansive and open, female energy is described as circumscribed and closed; this religion does not attach these qualities to the sex in question, nor does it attach any value judgments to energies deemed "negative" or "positive." The energies indicated just "are," without ascribing any value rooted like the sex itself. Energy is just energy in Ifá.

Interpreting the Lobes

Iya Obi divination starts with the lobes and the way they land on the divination tray (which is discussed next). Instrumental in interpretation are the markings on the lobe and the way they land. When the marking is visible after the lobe lands, it is read as "open." When not visible, it's interpreted as "closed." In the basic level of Iya Obi divination, the way the Iya Obi lobe falls is the whole story. In the more sophisticated levels of divination, the "sex" of the lobe comes into play, adding another layer of interpretation. At this level of divination, open sections are recorded as "O" and closed sections as "X."

Kola nuts are selected for divination when they are four-lobed but also at their freshest. When the nut has been around for a while, it can begin to crack, rendering the internal lobes visible. This nut cannot be used in divination.

The divination tray is used with the Iya Obi. Traditionally made of wood, the tray is elaborately carved by artisans dedicated to producing the sacred article. The intricate carvings are intended to honor the work of the priest.

The tray calls out to the Divine Messenger Elegua/Eshu to facilitate communication with Orunmila and through Orunmila, the other Orisha. The tray is covered with a white powder called "Iyerosun" (divining powder). This powder is produced by termites feasting on the Iyerosun tree. Without using this powder to the Opon Ifá, divination with the Opon Ifá cannot occur. Iyerosun is an integral component of the divination system of Ifá.

Opon Ifá, Spread with Iyerosun

Like the Opele, the Opon Ifá is used to discover the Odù (verse or story), indicated by the position of the Kola nut lobes when they fall and the movement of the Iyerosun dust resulting from the casting of the lobes.

Carvings around the perimeter of the Opon Ifá are more than just decorative. They indicate nine distinct sections to further support the interpretation of the Iya Obi and Iyerosun. Each of these sections represents the person of a revered ancient diviner.

The priest's job is to determine the Odù indicated by throwing nut lobes. The 256 Odù all have a place in divination, determined by the casting and marks made in the Iyerosun. The Odù indicated also determines the nature of the offerings to be applied to the problem the session addresses. The Odù is also associated with individual spirits and situations. Just as there are only a limited number of plot lines based on common human themes and problems, there are prototypical life challenges indicated by the Odù and sought in divination.

As mentioned earlier, the Opele is sometimes used in divination with the Opon Ifá. Opele is usually employed to discern the forward conduct of minor matters. Weightier problems and challenges are addressed by using the Iya Obi ikin.

A Blueprint for Living

The purpose of divination is the eventual perfection and purification of the human soul, refined in the practical and often challenging context of human life. Divination, the gift of OlOdù mare through the Oracle, Orunmila, is a link to Divine direction through the Orisha. Calling on the practice for guidance and self-reflection as a life discipline provides valuable information to better human life.

However, of all the characteristics of Ifá divination, perhaps the most genuinely surprising is guidance that is capable of changing the course of one's life. The Yoruba do not believe that the average human life is buffeted by the capricious winds of the universe—with notable exceptions like "spirit children," locked in a cycle of eternal immaturity. Instead, they believe that the individual is empowered to change the course of their life, taking charge by taking ownership.

This may sound suspiciously like the postmodernism assertion that we can create reality, but Ifá's philosophical framework and cosmology present the idea of self-empowerment differently. Divination answers human questions with the limitless experience of the Orisha, God's emissaries. Divination searches for the Odù that fits, and the questioning person seeks counsel and the answers sought. Yet those answers must be carried forward into life to represent genuine and profound change.

In Ifá, change is not optional when required. Change is the responsibility of the individual practitioner because what the individual does ripples outward, impacting the community's coherence and cohesion. Just as a pebble dropped in a puddle displaces and changes the water, so does the person resisting change. There is no excuse in Ifá for a refusal to follow the counsel of the learned Babalowa/Iyalawo, acting as a conduit to the spirit world. There is a commandment about that, if you recall.

While postmodernism counsels change for the benefit of the individual alone with no accommodation to anyone or anything, Ifá counsels change for the benefit of the individual in a material and spiritual community. In the material community, only goodness and decency retain the strength of the fabric. In the spiritual community of the Orisha and ancestors, the same is true. Individual action and challenges impact both halves of the cosmic gourd with equal force.

The divination work is much larger than any priest or community member seeking guidance and life improvement. It is bigger than discerning the way forward of the community in leadership or seeking the will of the Divine in matters of conflict and disharmony. The work of Orunmila's divinely inspired gift was of union between the two halves of the gourd, once separated by misbehavior, rudeness, and disregard for the dignity of the sacred.

Throughout life, Ifá practitioners build themselves into someone who is eventually remembered with affection and respect and welcomed by the world of spirits. Divination is the tool that draws this blueprint for living, spiritualizing the material and materializing the spiritual. Divination is the healing of Creation and the healing of human souls.

Chapter Five will discuss the casting of the ikin. You will find out how the Opon Ifá and the Iyerosun interpret the resulting configurations to arrive at the right Odù for the subject of the divination session.

Again, as a reminder, casting the ikin is not for the uninitiated (those who are not members of Ifá). Even those so initiated should also be initiated into the priesthood of the Babalawo/Iyalawo to practice divination. Please respect this ancient religion's tenets and prohibitions while enjoying your journey of discovery.

Chapter Five: How Ifá Is Cast and an Introduction to Odù Ifá

"Yoruba ethics: To become, through ritual, a being who knows more and understands more, a person who lives more and is more."

Ulli Beier

Something important to understand about divination and the interpretation of the ikin and Iyerosun is the Odù itself and what accompanies it. Many complex calculations must be made according to the casting signs on the Opon Ifá. These determine not only the Odù but also the gifts and sacrifices required to accomplish the effect or favor being sought.

Casting the kola nut lobes is a complicated, formulaic enterprise, demanding an impressive command of the used tools. There are many moving parts involved, and one of those moving parts is the Odù (which is discussed later)—the verse indicated by the casting. The application of the Odù to the problem being presented often helps the questioner connect the dots involved. The intervention of the Orisha through the Babalawo/Iyalawo and Eshu, the Divine Messenger, is mediated by the human priest. The priest reads, considers, and produces the Odù that has been spoken to him on the Opon Ifá.

This is not a "psychic reading." Ifá divination is a complex system of signs, prayer, praise, intention, ritual, and interpretation, requiring a sensitive diviner and a receptive supplicant, both focused on acquiring information that will move the individual—and thus the community—forward in spirit.

Preparing the Opon Ifá and Ikin

The priest and supplicant will be seated on the floor, and the Opon Ifá will sit before the Babalawo, with the "foot" of the tray nearest to him. The priest will be facing east. A tool used only in ikin/Opon Ifá divination, the iroke Ifá will be at the priest's side. This tapper will be used to summon Eshu and Orunmila by tapping it on the side of the Opon Ifá. This also calls forth the nine ancient revered diviners depicted around the edges of the Opon Ifá. The tray will have been spread with Iyerosun. This powder will be divided into nine sections corresponding to the nine great diviners. The Babalawo/Iyalawo will praise these revered ancestors.

Using the right hand, the ikin lobes will start to be packed in the priest's left hand. As there are sixteen in total, and they can be quite large, the kola nuts will begin to fall. When only one or two lobes are in the left hand, the priest is ready to cast. If more than two lobes remain, the packing process must be repeated until only one or two kola nut lobes remain.

Casting

The lobes are cast when only one or two kola nuts remain in the Babalawo/Iyalawo's hand. If one remains, the Iyerosun will be marked with two vertical strokes. If two, the powder will be inscribed with two vertical strokes.

This process is repeated eight times, resulting in various configurations that mean different things, directing the priest toward the appropriate Odù. This is determined by the markings made on the Opon Ifá, revealing the nature of the Odù. However, the supplicant's reason for seeking a divination session also figures in the priest's discernment.

When the left side of the Opon Ifá's markings matches those on the right side of the tray, the Odù is revealed. But these markings all refer to specific Odù, appearing in specific parts of the corpus of Ifá.

Names and symbols correspond to every Odù, with single lines denoting the "light" or open position and the double lines representing the "dark" or closed position (as discussed in the section on ikin in Chapter Four). However, there are two sets of signs produced in ikin casting.

The second set of symbols consists of the binary "0" and "1," with the 0 representing the "dark" or closed position and the 1 representing the "light" or open position. These are known as the "meji" Odù. This second set of signs is used only when the opele (divination chain) is used to cast.

The interpretation and process of casting may seem simple enough on the surface. But it is a complex matter that requires many years of training. As part of their initiation, priests must memorize the Odù Ifá.

With its 256 Odùs, this collection of spiritual knowledge expands and grows constantly. There is no canonization process, and, over time, some of the information contained in the Odù Ifá has been lost. However, revelation to the people is a continual thing. It does not stop when a hierarchical organization decides it should because the conversation between Olodumare and humanity is ongoing and eternal.

Within each of the 256 Odù are "ese," and there may be as many as 800 of these in every Odù. In the ese, the ongoing conversation is most vibrant, as these are added constantly to reflect new knowledge. For that reason, there is no accurate accounting of how many there are. Thus, imagine that the priest must commit all this information to memory to be prepared to provide supplicants with an accurate divination session. (See Resources for a link to a table with the symbols for every Odù in the Odù Ifá.)

Next, you will explore the Odù Ifá, what it means, and its role in Ifá divination.

The Odù Ifá

The understanding of Ifá is rooted in the Odù Ifá, a collection of parables and instructions that set out guidelines for ethical living. It is said that the Odù Ifá is a collection of binary codes (see the second set of symbols above, which are quite literally "0"s and "1"s). These codes express the totality of universal energy, coursing through the two halves of Ifá's cosmic gourd.

This energy gives life to all that lives, and within it resides every permutation of human life and its challenges. Fortune and misfortune, blessing and curse, birth and death, and everything in between are found in this book of ethical, moral, and spiritual wisdom.

The sixteen major Odù (Meji/Oju Odù) are first. The other 240 Odù are elaborations and commentary on the first sixteen. In the Odù are the keys to living well and the healthy spirituality that accompanies a well-lived life. The Odù are oracles in and of themselves.

Each Odù contains detailed information about solving the problems and challenges of life, with instructions as to how the supplicant is to approach the solution, including the attendant rituals, medicinal responses, and sacrifices required to affect a fitting response that pleases the Orisha.

In the ese contained in the Odù are poetic instructions directing followers to their obligations to the Orisha and the best course of action to resolve the problem or question brought to divination.

The Odù Ifá is not a codified (written) tradition. It is a large corpus of oral tradition, passed down from priest to priest and committed to memory. Any written expressions you see are secondary to the pure tradition of Ifá. And while there is an "app for that"—yes, a phone app—it is clear that such innovations are not in the spirit of this ancient religion.

The Blueprint behind the Blueprint

Odù Ifá, with its binary codes and energetic basis, serves as a blueprint for divination. While divination offers a blueprint itself, that blueprint evolves over time, with the Odù Ifá as its true foundation. Without the knowledge presented by the corpus of Yoruban wisdom, there is no point in divination. And without the Babalawo/Iyalawo, there is no knowledge. Without these two elements reaching out to the Orisha on behalf of the supplicant, there is no divination. It has no meaning.

Divination is a gateway to the knowledge through the spirit that Ifá is rooted in. As cornerstones of the faith, intelligence and wisdom are developed through the gift of divination, teaching, and admonishing the supplicant to know more and live more fully (see the quote at the start of this chapter). Intelligence and wisdom, supported by the Odù Ifá and its teachings and prescriptions, are the way to "Ori," the soul's destiny and path in life and death; the seat of intellect, wisdom, and spirituality. As the "head," the Ori stands in a similar position to the concept of free will in the Christian religion.

The spark of consciousness alive in the human being is the ability and the power to change the self to more closely resemble the Divine primordial vision. And in the Ori is the spiritual consciousness, working in concert with the intellect. When the Ori encounters Odù Ifá in divination, it is dignified and expanded, becoming the Orisha it is intended to be. The Ori is the "divine self," beyond the mere mortal human organism's presumed default settings. In fact, the Ori is an emanation of the Divine, giving it the status of a personal Orisha.

Orthopraxy

In the Ifá religion, orthopraxy is not just built into daily life in the Sixteen Commandments. It is implied by divination itself. When you ask someone for advice in a religious setting, and they go to great lengths to give it to you, ignoring that advice is an act of profound disrespect. And to insult or disrespect the Babalawo/Iyalawo is to break the Sixteenth Commandment (see Chapter One).

Orthopraxy, the "right action" that typifies the ideal Ifá life on earth, is played out in the very structure of the religion, guiding the practitioner closer to a spiritual ideal that serves both halves of the Divine gourd, bringing harmony in the actions of those who are learning to live well. Without reflection, there is no action, so orthopraxy is an action arising from and guided by reflection.

It might be said that orthopraxy has its foundation in wisdom. Having grown from the integration of thought and emotion in Ori, wisdom seeks the good in all things, practicing what it preaches by acting following what is right and good. These actions lead to the harmonious conduct of life by the individual in the surrounding community.

Moreover, in Ifá, the community is a microcosm of Creation itself, modeling the attributes of Olodumare, as expressed in the Orisha. All are brought together in orthopraxy when the talk becomes the walk.

In the Ifá religion, talk is constructive, not demonstrative. To talk is to explore solutions, instructions, and prescriptions. It is to share tradition toward the betterment of human life. It's not to sing of one's devotion. When the right action is the imperative of the community, talk is cheap. The action does all the talking, reifying belief as just behavior that gives more than it takes.

The Ancestors Speak

Collected in the corpus of the Odù Ifá is the wisdom of generation upon generation of Ifá believers. Refining and enhancing through time with new knowledge and insights, the living, growing nature of these verses is probably what is most extraordinary.

This oral tradition is vast, encompassing knowledge gathered over 8,000 years. This knowledge is assembled to guide practitioners with tools that have survived time to come to them as gifts of wisdom. Primarily, these are etiological (an explanation of why things are the way they are) and expository (explanations about how things happen and how to deal with them) narratives. Within those narratives are the archetypes represented by the Odù themselves, symbolizing the vast, untapped knowledge in the collective unconscious of humanity.

As we move forward in subsequent chapters to read more about the Odù Ifá, the simplicity and ethical soundness of its contents will become apparent. The Odù Ifá is the great blueprint of a life driven by the seeking after wisdom through the agency of the intellect. The priest can only share what has been divined. The diviner can only tell the supplicant what has been indicated on the Opon Ifá by the ikin or the opele.

Once the divination session has been accomplished, it is the supplicant's responsibility to act; to perform the orthopraxis demanded by the verses indicated, the urgings of the Orisha, and the work of the Babalawo/Iyalawo.

When the ancestors and Orisha speak through divination, the wisdom of experience accumulated over 8,000 years is laid out to the living. And that experience guides right action, helping the living live more authentically and less anxiously. The ultimate truth is that humanity is not created for its own sake but to bring harmony to a troubled Creation.

Chapter Six: Odù Ifá I, Part One — Ogbe and Oyeku

The remainder of this book focuses on the Odù Ifá, with each of the final seven chapters representing the four distinct sections of these teachings, with each section divided into two chapters for the sake of readability, save the last one, which is less complex.

Before we begin, it is helpful to think of the Odù as archetypes (in the Jungian sense). As you read about each chapter's function and its place in the lives of the Ifá faithful, know that the Ifá concept of consciousness is very similar to that proposed by Carl Jung. The Odù represent various energetic realities in the universe connected to consciousness. Like Jung's archetypes, the Odù are models existing in the collective unconscious, which are incomprehensible to us until the time we can absorb their message comes. The Odù are the energies that must be learned to understand one's destiny and humanity's collective destiny.

This chapter will cover the four sections noted above, starting with Ogbe (also referred to as Ejiogbe Oguna or Ogbe). Ogbe's teachings about Ori concern the practitioner's ability to heed the promptings of the intellect in spirit, guiding them in the right direction. When you can unquestioningly listen to these promptings, you are trusting what is known to most of us as "intuition."

The Ori, the seat of our destiny and intuitive sensing capacity, is the most important of all our faculties in the Ifá worldview. This is where answers may be sought and found, so Ogbe directly instructs Ifá adherents on how they might use what they have learned to heed Ori and trust it implicitly.

Ori — The Hidden Orisha

The Ori, that personal core where thought and emotion are processed to help us make decisions and make sense of life, is the divine kernel of the human being. In it, we see the tremendous potential of human intelligence. For this reason, it is an Orisha unto itself, defining our consciousness and its movement through the world.

This tells us that the divine kernel in the human being is the way toward our fullest potential. In Christianity, the soul is somewhat analogous to the idea of Ori but is not of the same stature. In Christianity, the soul is subject to God. In Ifá, the Ori acts as Divine Will filtered through the human intellect and spirit, becoming its own reflection of Divine Nature. However, the Ori is unique to the human animal. We are precious in the sight of the Divine and worthy to carry such an encouraging truth as the Ori within us. But the Ori is to be developed. It is deposited as a vessel of our efforts. Like the Christian concept of salvation, it is freely given but sanctified by the recipient's efforts of such a tremendous gift.

Yet, that does not mean Ori is born autonomous. It's trained to be so. It's a life's work to leverage the fullness of the Ori's capacity for orthopraxy and train the mind to understand what that is in any given situation. The Ori is a vessel of wisdom, guided by the work of divination, which leads the practitioner to the Odù Ifá and its multitudinous lessons for leading a life worthy of Olodumare's goodness.

Leadership 101

The teachings of Ogbe encompass the qualities humans tend to expect in a leader, counseling that we all have these qualities in an undeveloped form. While some people may model leadership naturally, that describes few people. Most of us need to learn what leadership looks like by encountering good examples of it.

Thus, with the priest as a guide, the practitioner attends to the Ori as a means of finding within it the qualities of leadership. Modeled by Olodumare, the priest, and the Orisha, the Ifá practitioner, is guided toward her capacity to model the qualities demanded of leaders to benefit family, community, and Creation itself.

The qualities of a leader, as interpreted by Ogbe, may be readily found in the Sixteen Commandments of Ifá, a thumbnail of the teachings of Odù Ifá. These sixteen basic teachings all encourage honesty, integrity, decency, humility, compassion, and empathy. The ideal leader has all these qualities and more to spare, so self-development becomes a goal to be the best version of yourself possible.

Patience Is the Start of Good Character

Take a quick look around, and you will see that most people are impatient and emotionally dysregulated. We act before we think. We throw tantrums when we do not get what we want, and our drive for instant gratification is constantly fed in a society driven by technological immediacy.

However, patience is the mark of someone who has learned that the alternative does not get you very far. When we are impatient, we say things we don't mean. We allow our emotions to get the better of us because we don't know how to control them. This leads to extreme social volatility, which is neither desirable nor necessary. The ability to control our emotions in the presence of triggers and stressors is one factor that keeps us from going off and suffering the consequences that follow. Without patience, we're like babies waking up from an afternoon nap, screaming over trivial matters like a slow barista or a late bus. When we have the patience required to wait for things to work out as they eventually will, we're in control of our emotions instead of allowing them to control us.

Temperance in All Things

The human temperament is an unruly beast, so Ifá rightly sets out to tame it, and it does so not with prohibitions but with prescriptions. While many of the Sixteen Commandments of Ifá have a distinct "don't" orientation, the net effect suggested by following them is entirely positive. And the work of Ogbe is similarly positive.

Temperance is an important factor in Ifa.
https://unsplash.com/photos/OptEsFuZwoQ

Temperance has more than health benefits for the human organism. It has a mediating effect on emotions by helping to maintain balance. When out of balance, we are out of sorts, out of patience, and into a whole new size of clothes! That is the problem with instant gratification. Patience demands that we wait to be gratified. It further demands that we still our impatience to wait for the best possible outcome. That outcome only arrives when we sit on the fidgeting toddler within.

The Self-Indulgence of Negativity

While we are living in an undoubtedly self-indulgent age, it is clear that many of us have always been that way. Humans tend to have a belief in the uniqueness of their experiences. We cling to this belief so passionately that we cannot imagine any other destiny than the one we have convinced ourselves is our birthright.

We have all had gifts and vocations, but even if this is the case, they are wasted when the will to employ them fruitfully is not present. We throw out the champagne, uncorked. There is brilliance in every Ori in every human being, but the self-indulgence of negativity can easily squash that brilliance.

Negativity is a type of egotism that demands that destiny conforms to worldly imperatives. However, the Ori is not mocked. Choosing not to listen to the Ori is, in Ifá, choosing to ignore the voices of the ancestors through the Babalawo/Iyalawo. It chooses the unreal over the real, the world over the spirit.

And in this choice is a return to the original division of the great gourd of the cosmos. We were cavalier. God was not amused, so Olodumare withdrew, putting a little distance between the Divine and material Creation. The rejection of the wisdom available to people in the Ifá tradition, for whatever reason, creates a small rupture in the relationship with Olodumare and the spirit world and, thus, with the ancestors. That is profoundly negative, affecting the community in its very fabric.

Even when born with an undeniably stellar destiny, there are people in this world who choose to wander aimlessly, looking for themselves in an external narrative. Yet, the true destiny of the individual is alive in the Ori, and when it is fed and fostered, acknowledged, and heeded, the Ifá follower grows to the Ori's full stature.

True leadership is not being a figurehead or a "top dog." True leadership is being a light among others and leading the way by deed and word. Our thoughts and emotions are integrated into Ori in growing wisdom; we are equipped to deploy our words and deeds to the good. When that is done consistently, we're leaders, lighting the way for others.

Obatala's Legacy

Obatala is described in the oriki (praise poetry) dedicated to him:

"He is patient.

He is silent.

Without anger, he pronounces his judgment."

And the virtue of patience toward just judgment, meditating on the factors involved, and dispensing deliberative justice, is how he is depicted. In this respect, the Ogbe of Odù Ifá stands as a description of the attributes of the co-creating Orisha— Olodumare's right-hand man, if you will. However, the oracle, Orunmila, is of a similar deliberative, patient temperament.

One of Ogbe's illustrative ese's tells of Orunmila's extraordinary patience. The Orisha is said to wait three years if offended. This, explains Orunmila, allows the transgressor to correct the offense given. Even when given to pass judgment, the oracular Orisha moves deliberately, measuring his steps not in time but awareness.

The fact that these two Orisha are so central to this chapter of Odù Ifá makes clear that the practitioner is being trained to contain visceral emotional responses after the example of two of the most prominent primordial Orisha. Neither acts precipitously, choosing slow, deliberate action that leads (logically) to well-founded decisions. Many wars might be avoided with such a robust moral framework in play.

The message of Ogbe is that the development of patience and emotional regulation is the foundation of Ori's true realization. When we have control of ourselves, we have control of the world around us, reacting with measured, thoughtful action. Leadership relies on such action and such a process of patient deliberation to pursue justice and orthopraxy.

The Objective of Patience

The Ogbe states:

> "*Nothing of any value is created by an uncontrolled temper.*
>
> *Patience is the foundation of existence.*
>
> *A patient person has the world.*
>
> *She will grow old in bliss.*
>
> *His health will be robust.*
>
> *She will live a life of happiness and enjoyment,*
>
> *With the taste of honey on her tongue."*

As with most of the proscriptions and prescriptions we read in Chapter One's review of the Sixteen Commandments, the reward of good is in doing good, and the reward of patience is in the ripe fruit it bears.

Reaching up to pluck an apple from a tree that has not ripened is no victory. It cannot be eaten with pleasure. But the wise person whom Ori counsels that the apple must be left to ripen eats with pleasure when the fruit is ready to be enjoyed in its full delight.

The fruit of patience is the same—patience blooms with time and practice. We learn to contain our reactions. We learn to examine the moment with clear eyes, seeing all around us. We learn to be human in a way that honors the gift of being born to this legacy of our Ori's guidance through the world.

Patience is at the heart of emotional regulation. When we learn to examine our emotions, assigning them the value they deserve and nurturing them as part of us, we acknowledge them. At the same time, we put them in their place, knowing they can be dangerous influences when left unexamined. With our emotions in our command by virtue of our intellect, we can more readily step out into the world in the confidence that we're not going to lose it today, that we're going to be aware, informed humans. We walk in the confidence of the evolved self when we command our emotions and understand our thoughts.

Leadership is in the living of its role among human communities—the modeling of a way to live together in harmony, free of rancor and unnecessary competition. It is how we treat others, never leading astray or saying what we know not to be true. These simple rules for living are the social connective tissue that binds us together in love, leading one another to a less stressful way of living together.

In that binding is the reconstruction of our relationship with Olodmare.

Oyeku

Oyeku is the very heart of the darkness of the void—that which we do not know but will someday. It is the beginning and the end of all things.

Oyeku means death, but it means so much more. Oyeku is the unknown eternality of things. We are unconscious of it unless we are philosophers or students of religion. However, even such people cannot hope to penetrate the fullness of the mystery that is Oyeku. That is for the spirit world and those who inhabit it.

In Oyeku is the journey of life, unfolding eternally and simultaneously, in a place with no time, no space as we know it, no materiality, and no passions. Time has one meaning here—the cycles of life just turn. Those cycles are many in our lives, made cycle after cycle. Those cycles teach us how to prepare the soul for the greatest adventure of all: Death.

The Circle Is Unbroken

To seek commonalities in the philosophical underpinnings of the world's religions is not to seek integration or syncretization; rather, it is to understand how deeply ingrained in human thinking the circular model of time is.

We live in a circular, cyclically bound cultural setting, wherever we are. Assumptions are made about how we shall live depending on age, sex, attractiveness, and intellectual ability. In almost every society, birth is followed by some form of education, then marriage, then offspring. These milestones represent cycles that we are compelled to realize—whether they are appropriate for us or not—because there was a period before the recorded time when our survival depended on the realization of these milestones.

Reflecting on the concept of Oyeku frees the intellect to apprehend destiny as part of that dark reality. In Oyeku is an unknown that may be known. But not now. To truly be in the unbroken circle of life, we must be awake to all of it, including the inevitability of death.

To the Ifá, death is not the unknown but part of the life we know. Thus, death continues this life, taking with us all we have learned in our spiritual journeys to the spirit world, just as the ancestors did before us. In Ifá, it is thought that only the ignorant fear death. The learned and integrated person, connected to their Ori, does not fear death but approaches it mindfully. They step carefully toward that horizon that never arrives, aware, awake, and ready for the next chapter and the chapter after that.

To be ready for death—no matter when it comes—is to be ready to know Oyeku, this womb of nothingness and progenitor of life's cycles. Without fear, the Ifá respectfully and consciously approach her hallowed precincts. All things begin, and all things end. These realities are part of living a conscious, dignified, and satisfying life. Both beginnings and endings are good because nothing ever truly ends.

This chapter has covered some key concepts and features of Ifá that will help you contextualize the content of subsequent chapters, giving you a brief grounding of Ifá's core ideas and how they are presented in the Odù Ifá.

The four sections of the Odùe Ifá covered in this part of the book have been broken into two chapters each. The next chapter covers the next two Odù s of Odù Ifá I.

Chapter Seven: Odù Ifá I, Part Two — Iwori and Odi

This chapter will explore Part Two of Odù Ifá I in the Odù s of Iwori and Odi and their energetic roles in the teachings imparted by divination.

Iwori

Iwori is another tremendously profound metaphysical concept that has to do with consciousness. In Ifá, everything that exists has a type of consciousness. It may not be like human consciousness, but it is consciousness nonetheless.

Iwori is a penetrating gaze, discerning consciousness as an entity unique to the bearer, seeing the process of consciousness itself as one of individualization. In practice, Iwori is transformation, a feat accomplished by applying fire. In the case of Iwori, that fire is passion.

Passion has many faces. They are not all pretty. Passion can lead to the birth of children, sanctified partnerships, and the accomplishment of great change. However, passion can also lead to conflict, even the extreme war conflict. Thus, to understand Iwori, we should understand transformation as being wrought in the fire of passion, but the passion generating the fire is mindful. This is not the unbridled passion that passes after the heat of the moment has subsided. Transformation is sustained fire. The fire of passion, like the material fire in which gold may not be eliminated but only refined, reveals the purity of the soul.

Individualization and Consciousness

Ori is the key to arriving at an understanding of Iwori. The Ori, as discussed in the last chapter, is both consciousness and the destiny of that consciousness. It is the seat of the soul and our self-concept. With divination, Ori is tried as a precious metal—by the fire of passion that leads to transformation.

It is Iwori that most directly confronts Ori. Through its penetrating gaze, Iwori reaches toward the Ori with the fire it needs to be transformed. This is the Divine gaze that knows us and is part of us simultaneously, with the Ori as its throne in the human body. Iwori links our consciousness/destiny and the spirit world and the Divine.

The individualized unit of consciousness is, of course, the human being. We are this consciousness, enfleshed because we perceive ourselves. We are self-conscious and aware that we are we. I am me. You are you. We know ourselves as units of consciousness, moving through the world in the borderland of flesh that defines us as the human organism, making us intelligible to those we encounter in the world.

Our flesh, acted upon by our consciousness, is how we know the world around us. We touch, taste, smell, hear, and see the world in our senses. In our consciousness, we interpret the senses as received. However, it is all one thing, working as a single unit of consciousness. The flesh communicates to the consciousness the sensation, flavor, scent, sound, and sight we experience, revealing it as information to be interpreted.

For Ifá, this is all learning, feeding the Ori. That feeding is accompanied by the gift of divination, further feeding the Ori. The fire is born in the interaction of the individual with the truths of life revealed to him in Odù Ifá. The supplicant is given a choice in divination—to be alive to the guidance of the Orisha or to shrink from it. Yet, as discussed, it is not really a choice at all when you think of what is to be gained by building on the lessons of divination translated to orthopraxy.

The Fire of Transformation

Iwori, that penetrating gaze, brings the fire to the soul by any number of means. Learning is chief among them, but sometimes, people need to feel the fire before learning. That can be transforming, too. Adversity is often transformative. Sometimes bad things happen to good people, especially in Ifá, so they can learn something important.

Because of our individualized consciousness, human beings experience the world in myriad ways. What is fascinating for one is tedious for another. What brings happiness to you brings misery to someone else. This person-to-person individualization of consciousness is leveraged in Ifá to speak directly to the Ori. The uniqueness of the Ori in each person is the proving ground of a life lived mindfully, spiritually, and in community with other, individualized units of consciousness.

Look around and ask yourself what is at the heart of most Western societal problems. For some, it is the elevation of the individual above all considerations. What the individual chooses to do has more weight than what the community needs the individual to do. We can see this most clearly in resistance to the COVID vaccine.

The individualized consciousness, aware of itself and other units of consciousness, is potential. In Ifá, that potential is to be deployed toward the cohesion of the community, rooted in tradition, guided by divination and the Odù Ifá. It is not expressly for itself. Rather, it recognizes that the whole is greater than a component thereof.

A Conscious Universe?

As stated earlier, the Ifá viewpoint is that everything in Creation has consciousness. But what if the universe itself was conscious? Emerging research is asking that very question.

Ifa questions the consciousness of the universe.
https://unsplash.com/photos/oMpAz-DN-9I

Materialism has been the predominant scientific explanation for consciousness—that consciousness emanates from activity in the brain. The Platonic/Cartesian mind-body split is favored—consciousness is separate from the body, existing independently as the "soul." Now, enter panpsychism, which posits a consciousness inhabiting every fiber of the universe.

As it observes what is around us, our individualized consciousness is separate yet contained in this universal consciousness, giving awareness to every material thing. Biological organisms—including us—continually make decisions rooted in consciousness without even thinking about it. When confronted with a stairway, we climb. When confronted with a wall, we find a way to get around it. We change our behavior to accommodate what we have encountered in the world. These automated decisions concerning physical navigation are consciousness, too.

Moreover, while panpsychism continues to be a marginal theory of consciousness, the idea of consciousness found "out there, somewhere" and "everywhere there is" points to Iwori. The penetrating gaze of consciousness outside ourselves, observing and interacting with our individualized consciousness, may sound like science fiction. However, in the world of discerning humanity's relationship to spirit, Iwori as a function of universal consciousness seems plausible. While speculative, panpsychism changes the channel of our understanding of consciousness, which does not seem to be able to formulate a definitive response about what it is.

Perhaps consciousness—the universal kind, external to our units of consciousness—is the penetrating gaze of Iwori, inviting us to transform. In that gaze is the fire of passion, urging humanity toward a spirituality that is equally penetrating, binding all consciousness together in a singular purpose.

Ministering to the Ori, Iwori's gaze is laser-focused, producing the spark that will provoke the conflagration that burns away all that is unworthy, liberating it to proceed toward its destiny in awareness. Awareness, then, is the gift that is transformed because if the universe is consciousness, we are its spiritual messengers through the Divine Ori.

Our thoughts and emotions integrated, we are transformed under the penetrating gaze of Iwori, emerging as the Divine image Obatala once wreaked in us. Animated by the breath of Olodumare, we are ignited in the glare of Iwori's challenge to transform, reborn in passion as a fully realized human being.

Odi

Cyclical time means that all is eventually reborn, in one way or another. In Ifá, the concept of reincarnation (Atunwa) is also present as a rebirth within a life cycle and into a new and separate life cycle with its own identity.

In Ifá, nothing is created or destroyed in the natural world. Rather, all that is has been transformed from something else and will be again, in a continuous cycle of rebirth. The perfect example is the one discussed earlier—the creation of humanity. Obatala made the forms of primordial human beings from clay.

As in the Biblical Creation narrative, water was mixed with the earth's dirt and molded to create a kind of homunculus, a representation of what was to be transformed by the breath of Olodumare. In this instance, the transformation of the substance is accomplished by the Divine breath and the implantation of the Ori, the Divine kernel within humanity.

Yet, Odi also represents the physical act of birthing and female reproductive organs, referring to the animal reality of reproduction and the nurturing of new life within the human female's body. The womb is the place of transformation in which something that exists is changed to become something else entirely.

This womb is Odi, where all is reborn eternally and simultaneously, confounding the Western concept of time and a fixed moment of creative action on the part of the Divine. In the world of the Odi, creation is ongoing and uninterrupted, its primordial layer only the beginning of the Divine project of transforming matter into something new. The implication is progressive improvement and perfection. Matter that is not serving its purpose is transmuted. It becomes something new, improved, and closer to fulfilling its original purpose as laid out in the mind of Olodumare.

Iwori and Odi

While Iwori tends to a purely metaphysical characterization, Odi adds carnality in the presence of the womb. Representing both physical birth and continual cycles of rebirth, Odi connects reincarnation (re-fleshing) as linked to conventional physical birth and possibly even analogous to it.

Iwori transforms via the Ori, and Odi does the same but with a markedly different focus. While Iwori's gaze sparks transformation in the individual, Odi represents all birth and rebirth and the cyclical nature of time. As part of this schema, reincarnation is inevitable as only one consideration to consider while reflecting on the nature of rebirth as an eternal, unbroken series of cycles.

These circles of time revolve even in the world of linear time. Each minute contains 60 seconds; each hour 60 minutes. Each follows the next, with the week ending in Omega and beginning the next day in Alpha. While we may not acknowledge this reality, it is clear that time is cyclical. Even if we do not want that to be true, disguising time's circular, cyclical nature with all manner of fancy dress worthy of a naked Emperor, it's clear we know on some level that cyclical is what time has always been.

As Odi presides over our endless, eternal cycles, Iwori transforms the transformed, perfecting and refining human potential as it moves through time, ever-revolving and evolving, growing, and shrinking, being born and dying. Because no state of being is fixed in this model, all of life is a transformation process governed by Divine imperatives characterized as metaphysical concepts —and in Odi's case, a physical hybrid.

Both Iwori and Odi are concerned with transformation but in distinctly different ways. Iwori's penetrating gaze transforms by ignition of the Ori in its integrated state. Odi, on the other hand, recycles, recreating everything that exists anew in all the cycles of its life. This is as true of human beings as anything else in Creation.

Odi is "the seal," representing the female reproductive organs. However, those organs are only the "accident"—the mask that conceals the true face of the form in Aristotelian thinking— beneath which the truth rests, awaiting exposure. The accident reminds us of the function of the form. Because in the case of Odi, we are talking about cyclical rebirth or transformation, the seal of Odi provides a convenient symbol for the cycles of life and the earth. The process of rebirth is a transformation of another kind. While the transformation of Iwori is a fire, bending but not breaking the stuff of humanity, it eternally works the human soul through its destiny.

In the question of transformation, Odi's womb is life itself. But it is also the mind of Olodumare, in which Creation is conceived and then born, midwifed into being by co-creator, Obatala.

Rethink, Recycle, Rebirth

In Ifá cosmology, all is reborn. Starting at the moment of Creation, nothing is static. Nothing is complete. Nothing is perfected, and everything is subject to change. Unlike the Biblical Creation account, Ifá admits that Creation was formed from existing substance. The raw material was there. However, as with the forms of humans created by Obatala, the breath of the Divine was required to animate it.

Thus, Odi stands as the Divine imperative to rethink, recycle, and rebirth as an eternal renovation project, ever perfecting what is. Just as human followers of Ifá seek to perfect themselves by integrating their thoughts and emotions toward regulation and seeking the advice of the Orisha, all Creation is a work in progress. Eternity is long, so there is no excuse not to choose devotion to self-improvement. Because every transformation you make is a transformation that impacts the whole, when all Creation is engaged in the act of eternal transformation, there's no static field. Change is inevitable and mandated by the Creator as the whole truth about Creation—that the Creator's work is never done.

Iwori's gaze penetrates the cycles of this life. We continue to transform and become the people we seek to be in this life. In the lives to come, Odi is the womb from which we continually spring, ever perfecting and participating in perfection as subjects of an evolving Creation.

You will recall that we discussed the evolving nature of Odù Ifá in Chapter Six, with ese being added as the Orisha speak to the Babalawos/Iyalawos, revealing more about the relationship between Olodumare and the people of Ifá. Like the Ifá model of Creation, nothing is written in stone. Nothing is ever written down. It is memorized, added to, reinterpreted, and recast, ever-transforming as we transform.

The world of Ifá and its complex thought is governed by change, improvement, and transformation that move the material world closer to the intended model of Olodumare. In this process, humanity acts as co-creator, fitting the two halves of the great gourd back together. That wholeness is the intended relationship.

It is the realization of Olodumare's dreams and eternal building project of humanity at the side of the Divine in common purpose.

Atunwa — The Recycled Soul

The concept of reincarnation in Ifá is very different from our conception in the West, which follows a loosely Eastern model. For us, reincarnation means returning to the earthly plane—whether consciously or unconsciously—as an ethereal soul inhabiting other people's bodies in other ages. This process is said to mitigate karmic obligations accumulated, leading us to Nirvana (the soul's perfection and release from "samsara"—the existential wheel).

In Ifá, the concept of reincarnation is rooted in individual choice. The Ori, the seat of the intellect and destiny, is the seat of this choice. This is the goal of divination—to illuminate the sacred Ori (the Orisha within) with the limitless wisdom of the spirit world. In pursuing the directives and guidance of divination, Ifá followers learn how to live in fidelity to their revealed destiny, fostering its direction and nurturing their understanding of it.

The ideal of Ifá, as in many other religions, is abundance, happiness, and a long life lived well. But that can only happen in Ifá when the practitioner is in tune with the Ori and the destiny it encapsulates. In this life, we choose our destinies by following the Sixteen Commandments. We heed the work of divination and the guidance of the Orisha through the Babalawo/Iyalawo. In following faithfully and practicing the orthopraxy prescribed by divination, the practitioner's soul is transformed, prepared for the reality of Atunwa and the destined evolution of the soul.

In the soul's future journey, the transformation of Odi, both physical and metaphysical, joins the work of Iwori, recycling and reusing the eternal soul. Duly formed in material life, the soul ventures forward into lives unknown, both in spirit and body. The mystery of a Creation that is ongoing, eternal, and cyclical is a journey of the human soul through the cycles of time, bound to sub-cycles that govern the conduct of that soul. Revolving and evolving, Atunwa is humanity's partnership with time, the soul submitting to the reality of Atunwa as the nature of the Created Order. Never completed, ever-evolving, all that is created is endlessly perfected and eternally ignited by the fire that changes but does not destroy.

Next, let us move into the second section of the Odù Ifá, reviewing the first two of the group in the next chapter.

Chapter Eight: Odù Ifá II, Part One — Irosun and Oronwin

The framework of destiny is known in the Ori and revealed through the practice of divination. However, the realization of destiny is embodied by the practitioner. We choose to realize our potential or choose to reject it. That brings us to Irosun, the Odù of potential's fulfillment.

Irosun

Irosun concerns with the bold realization of potential, but it also means multiplication and increases. What is being increased is understanding, the qualities prescribed in the Sixteen Commandments, and the follower's adherence to the Ori's promptings. Once transformed by the fiery gaze of Iwori in submission to the cyclical leadings of Odi, Irosun goads the follower toward increase/multiplication.

Increase/multiplication can mean anything, and depending on the cycle of life we find ourselves in, different priorities at different times. We might find a cycle of increase applies to money, wisdom, knowledge, patience, compassion, or holiness. Ori's urgings may remind us of areas we need to increase toward realizing our destiny at any point in our lives. Potential has many faces in human life. We model it in many ways, from physical strength to intelligence. Moreover, in Irosun, we meet the archetype who reminds us that our potential is never entirely realized. Eternity, remember, is a long time; however, that does not imply there is any sitting on our Irosun laurels!

Ori will make sure of that, and to keep pace with Ori, in fidelity to the destiny it is the guardian of, followers of Ifá are ever urged to "check themselves." Irosun implies that seeking potential in ourselves is how we push ourselves toward destiny and our work with the Divine. It's easy to become spiritually stagnant in many religious systems. But in Ifá, the driving force of divination and its connection to Ori creates a purpose-built vehicle that prevents such stagnation. The believer is part of a system that seeks communal orthopraxy within a religious framework. It's about what you think and what you do due to what you think. It's very much a works-based religion, demanding something from followers toward enhancing the whole, including the other half of the gourd, the spirit world.

The Blood

What Irosun also means in Yoruba is "menstrual blood." In that blood, present in its monthly cycles, is an elaboration on Atunwa because Atunwa means a specific type of reincarnation in Ifá, linked to the ancestors through the bonds of flesh (and blood).

While reincarnation is not strictly linked to family ties, Ifá says this is usually the case, with Atunwa primarily limited to family. The blood that once flowed through the ancestors' veins, in this way, is perpetuated. And the bonds of family are, as well. Blood is potential, and that is especially true of menstrual blood.

Menstrual blood is the cyclical shedding of the womb's lining, occurring on twenty-one to twenty-eight-day cycles throughout a woman's life from adolescence to menopause. Descending from Odi (the womb), this blood enters the material world as potential. When the blood does not come as it usually does, another kind of potential is being realized—that of birth.

Family blood and menstrual blood coalesce in Irosun as the ink creating the soul's road map to and through eternity. In blood is the stuff of life. In blood is the DNA of family lineage. And in the blood is the material maternal home of the soul in transit, ready to be born.

As we are talking about menstrual blood, we must also talk about women and their role in the life of Ifá. There is a remarkable contrast between the metaphor of menstrual blood as a symbol of potential in Ifá and the horror with which it is greeted in the Monotheistic Faiths. Without much detail, the Hebrew women of the Bronze Age were relegated to tents when they menstruated. And the Christian Church persisted in rites to "re-church" women after birth, as though birth had somehow sullied their bodies, well into the 1980s and later (see resources). While routinely framed as a "blessing," the churching of women was concerned primarily with ritual purity after its predecessor: Faith.

The positioning of women as metaphors for potential and the cyclical nature of life is a primordial response to women's reproductive functions, one of which is menstruation. While viewed as contaminating in some religious traditions, in Ifá, menstruation is viewed as a partner in the progress of time itself. A metaphor for time's cyclical nature, the potential of the blood is human—spiritually, intellectually, and materially. This conforms to a much older tradition of framing the female sex. Mysteriously bringing forth life in humanity's earliest days, women were viewed with reverence and fear. Whatever made the sunrise and set, it seemed too early for humans that women probably had something to do with it. The goddesses of the world's ancient cultures and the female Orisha speak to the power once held in menstrual blood and women as bearers of life. This ancient value in Ifá frames "woman" as the human embodiment of potential, stewards of both the womb and the blood that issues from it, representing potential and renewal.

Irosun has a negative side and, as usual, has to do with resisting one's destiny. When the practitioner works against the destiny outlined in the Ori and discovers in divination, the potential is choked off. Potential is refused. Even the blood of one's family and the ancestors' guidance is refused. However, who could refuse the riches of the past, present, and future in the potential the Ori holds as Divine legacy? It seems foolhardy, and perhaps that answers any questions about how it is that Ifá has survived eight millennia as a system of Faith. What works for people is usually continued, creating and recreating, birthing potential, and reincarnating it in Atunwa.

Potential in Flesh and Blood

Ifá's dedication to the community and the families that constitute it is clear in the conception of reincarnation in Atunwa. Blood is the potential of the flesh. The incarnation of potential relies on blood that springs from a font of relatedness. In this, the ancestors are serviced.

But all blood is potential in Irosun. The menstrual blood being the potential for life shed each month, is tied to the cycles of Creation, making Irosun that living womb of all lives that are, have been, and will be.

Inseparable from the living being, except in the monthly shedding of the womb's lining, the blood is the potential for graduation from the earthly to the spiritual. In the incarnate human is the potential for an eternity of spiritual evolution. This evolution is served both in the living human's development and the development of the soul liberated to its destiny in Atunwa.

Oronwin

Because the Odù Ifá's role is to define existence and the energies impacting it, members of the Faith are prepared for all contingencies, including the unexpected. This is the archetype of life represented by Orunwin—sudden, unexpected change.

This is where the Odù Ifá veers into the realm of Physics, specifically, the chaos that is matter's underlying nature. While we all like to believe that the universe, the world, and our lives are well ordered, Physics teaches that the truth is very different. The closer we examine the surface of things, the more chaos is seen beneath its flimsy veneer. Yet the more distance we place between ourselves and apparently unrelated, random events, the more orderly they appear. This is the effect described by Orunwin, which teaches perspective and the laudable trait of equanimity. Orunwin also instructs that all is not what it seems, demanding that the observer consider what is being experienced from the standpoint of impassive observation.

Our overthinking makes us see the chaos beneath the surface when we obsess about unexpected events—life's curveballs. In our zeal to make a difficult or unpleasant situation "go away," we major in the minors, picking problems apart until there is nothing left to pick, yet being no closer to any solution.

Alternatively, putting some distance between ourselves and what's happening allows us to see things as they are. What might appear chaotic up close will seem less so when viewed with detachment and realism.

Chaos Theory according to the Ifá

Chaos Theory (a branch of mathematics) proposes that combined chaos and order are the whole truth about reality. As stated above, what looks chaotic in proximity looks orderly from a distance. However, when chaos is considered from a mathematical perspective, the universe unfolds as it should, following a determined pathway that we perceive as chaos. But that is because we do not understand what we are looking at without doing the math.

The systems of the natural world are deeply deterministic. Yet, small changes to those systems can produce adverse effects over time. The Butterfly Effect, first described by meteorologist Edward Lorenz in 1961, analogizes this effect. Lorenz found that even minute errors in calculations when forecasting the weather threw the entire system out of whack. Just as a butterfly flapping its wings halfway around the world might be responsible for a hurricane, deviations in orderly systems can create ever-accumulating anomalies that result in similar disruptions.

Similarly, small disruptions of the destiny contained in the Ori of the individual threaten the integrity of the destiny's trajectory. The butterfly wings that buffet the world's stability are also capable of causing chaos in our lives—at least it looks like chaos, close up. The chaos just beneath the surface of life, the little bumps and grinds that distress and confuse us, is order asserting itself in ways we cannot predict. The death of a loved one, a sudden layoff from work, illness, and betrayal are part of life but appear to us as chaotic interruptions in our personal, calmly flowing rivers.

According to the Ifá, Chaos Theory is the peaceful meeting of life where it stands, understanding that everything happens as part of our destiny. Observed for what they are, the shocks of life are absorbed. When we look at what has happened in our lives as part of a greater story, not a personal insult or a life-destroying catastrophe, we're better able to see the order in chaos and, conversely, the chaos that serves order.

Returning to the Sixteen Commandments of Ifá, it is clear that their object is not orthopraxy for its own sake or for that of some arcane ideology—which is of little interest to the practice of Ifá. Instead, the Sixteen Commandments serve order by urging the faithful to act toward the smooth functioning of the communal system by avoiding disruptive behaviors because, in the model of the commandments, chaos is provoked by deviations in the conduct of life that creates hurt, misunderstanding, and even violence.

While under the calm surface of an orderly society, chaos teems as it serves that order, ever moving toward the solutions it was intended to create, its perceived presence in our lives is still serving that same order—in death, misfortune, illness, job loss, and disappointment. These contingencies are not essentially chaotic; they are simply part of an orderly reality in which chaos is part of a whole, reproducing reality as we know it.

Change and Equanimity

Oronwin provides perspective to supplicants who come to divination in times of flux and upheaval. Change means different things to different people. Some people provoke change voluntarily, knowing that change is needed. However, most of us find change threatening. We are creatures who like the familiar. A two-week vacation is just about right for most of us. Most of us want to return to our own beds after a vacation—too much change.

Change demands adaptation. When it is an unforeseen change of whatever kind, the ability to confront it makes us resilient. We learn from surviving, not from contentment. Contentment is the reward you receive for surviving.

Increasingly, societies everywhere have become less resilient due to an unwillingness to absorb change by adapting to it. Change and adaptation can take numerous forms, from personal tragedy to natural disasters. But to survive, we must be prepared to accept change as a challenge.

We adapt to changing from the comfort and dependence of childhood to transition into the adult world. This transition is common to all of us, with exceptions to the rule that only serve to prove it. Yet, when a change arises like a pandemic, do we accept the temporary inconvenience represented by mandates to mask or distance socially, or do we rebel against them? Which is the more common response?

Fortunately, most choose acceptance in the face of change, which comes with the inconvenience. That is how we survive. Even if we find the change abhorrent (occupation, war), we must learn to be in the experience as ourselves, fully engaged with the moment and not attempting to disrupt it with personal interest. In moments of great change, there is no personal interest. There's communal integrity that serves the desired outcome: Survival.

The perspective offered by Orunwin concerning change is that of equanimity. Change will happen. It is inevitable—and the choices you make when determining fidelity to the destiny held within the Ori. Thus, Orunwin counsels the type of acceptance that invests the mind in its own happiness. This is equanimity.

Equanimity places the person's response above the disruption encountered in the magnitude of importance. It is not the condition that matters where equanimity is concerned; it's the individual's response to that condition. All things have equal value in life and must be seen as parts of a whole which is the big picture.

The ancient Stoics believed that equanimity brought happiness, placing its practice high on its list of personal virtues, and virtue, they believed, was enough to keep you happy. This is similar to the idea of Oronwin in the Odù Ifá. Oronwin is the energy of change, and the change in Ifá is a challenge—a rite of passage that demands a response indicating your maturity as a human being. That maturity, in Orunwin, is seen in the ability to step back and consider the place of each change in life, whether cyclical (adulthood, birth, death, marriage) or unique incidents (sudden economic or social loss, accidents, ill-health). This is summed up in the character trait of equanimity.

Ifá's teachings in the archetypes expressed in the Odù Ifá are oriented toward self-command and exemplary action. Orthopraxy being central to the practice of the religion is only possible in a person who has learned what it is to be genuinely and deeply human. In Ifá, that deep humanity is the centrality of the spirit in incarnated life. The Ori must be followed, the intellect developed, and the spirit attuned to its destiny to serve that spirit. That destiny is to serve the whole great gourd.

Imagine the Ifá concept of Atunwa for a moment. Imagine the cycles of life being eternal with the souls of the Faithful learning through eternity, acting justly through eternity, and adding ese to the Odù Ifá through eternity. Change is part of these life cycles after life, simultaneous and yet, removed. Change is the nature of life, with the death of the physical body being the greatest change we will ever experience after that first moment outside the birth canal, dripping with Irosun's potential.

A Big Change

Death is feared by most of us. It is the unknown, and, like change, humans are not crazy about what they do not know or understand. However, like all the other life changes, death must be accepted. One has no alternative. Death is the end.

Thus, equanimity becomes Ifá's means of teaching the Faithful about the biggest change of all, the death of the material body. In Ifá, there's no dichotomy between the body and spirit. The spirit of humanity is divinely implanted as a part of the body. It is unique to the individual and not fixed. On the contrary, an individual's destiny may be changed due to their actions. The Ori of an individual may be improved or degraded. It is entirely the individual's decision what to do about themselves. But the best choice is made abundantly clear to the practitioner by the community around them and the people in it.

In the metaphors and ideas explored in this chapter, you have discovered a practical and constructive heart to the Ifá faith and the ultimate gift of divination. The Odù Ifá's lessons in Irosun and Oronwin are about the cycle of life itself, reaching out to the individual member to prepare them in this life for all that will come. In all our cycles, we honor and increase our potential. And in all our eternities, we change and transform profoundly.

Chapter Nine: Odù Ifá II, Part Two — Obara and Okanran

In this, we come to the concept of inner character. Starting with Obara (strength) and concluding with Okanran (humility), there is an interplay between the two qualities we can all learn something powerful from.

Obara

Strength can be a confusing term, muddled with culture. For some, it means winning at all costs and coming out on top; collateral damage damned. However, that is the negative face of Obara, the Odù/archetype of strength. In Ifá, the ego is born in the will to personal power, which precludes humility.

The imposition of one's will to prevail is the opposite of humility, which seeks its place among many. Ego demands its place above all. It is easy to see this in community elevation in the Ifá Faith, but in Ifá, Obara is also the birthplace of humility.

Having already irritated Olodumare with their rude, dismissive habits, human beings would be best served by not mistaking strength for self-interest. For nothing in Ifá may be had at the expense of others when the religion's Commandments are followed. And no living human being can ever match the strength of the Creator.

Yet, humanity can be a bit pigheaded, so the idea that we are "bigger than God" pervades at certain moments, leading us to behave irrationally and counter to reality. It's difficult for us to concede that the heavens are not solely concerned with us, personally. We cannot help believing, it seems, that nature was created solely for our cavalier use.

Egotism is anathema to the practice of Ifá for all the reasons you have been reading about. Odù Ifá, working in tandem with Ifá divination practices, is intended to divest followers of this all-too-human tendency, replacing it with the true strength of which Obara is the universal archetype. When the elevation of the self is reformed, humility has space to develop. But only when this transformation takes place can that true strength take root.

The Strength to Confront Reality

Lately, the reality is something else we humans do not seem to much care for. And yet, there it is: The elephant in the room, relieving itself of all our confabulating fun. However, the reality is the truth, and we may only be transformed by that truth by confronting it.

Confronting reality is perhaps the birthplace of the equanimity we read of in the last chapter, where the rubber meets the road, and we accept change by keeping calm and carrying on. It is a scary thing to do, but we all must confront reality. We need to admit that life does not always run as though on a conveyor belt, conveniently sending us off on our way in only one predictable direction. We need to make peace with the fact that we will die, we are finite, and our fleshly existence is not the nexus of reality.

We must confront and discern reality for the demands of a future of well-developed equanimity. Learning that you cannot always get what you want takes longer for some than others. But learn you must to survive and thrive and graduate through the cycles of your eternal life to spiritual maturity. And within Obara is the answer, which is the transformation of the ego, making space for humility to arise and overwhelm it. This is one of the principal lessons of life for the Ifá. Humility is at the center of their practice as the connective tissue of a communally ordered society.

Character Is Humility

Only when the ego is tamed can space for humility be made. The ego has sharp elbows, demanding as much space as possible. Ego spreads, making a two-seater on the bus a one-seater.

When the ego is duly tamed, it is contained to its rightful place, not spreading out to command more space than it's due but ordered and managed to make space for humility. As you read earlier, humility is a key human characteristic prized in Ifá. Humility causes us to consider the other side of arguments, take other people's concerns seriously, and factor their right to peace and well-being into our words and actions.

Humility is the core of a good character, engaged with the project of being decent, respectful, and considerate of the needs of others. When ego spreads itself out, taking up more space than a single person has any right to, there is no space for humility, self-reflection, or self-correction. Humility is elbowed out.

In Okanran, we explore the universal energy of humility and how its formation depends on knowing Obara well and realistically.

Okanran

In Ifá, tutu represents the balancing of emotion and thought. This is required to free human beings from the mindlessness of the lizard brain (the amygdala), which is the reactive, primitive part of the brain. When tutu is achieved, thoughts and emotions inform one another, with thought tempering emotion and vice versa.

The perfect illustration of what happens when thought and emotion are disconnected is found in the Third Reich. As the extermination of those deemed "the enemy" was the goal, the enemy's dehumanization was required to meet that goal. To do this, the Nazis engaged in the intellectualization of genocide, rejecting any emotional input as to the humanity of the people they were torturing and killing.

When the intellect is unmoored from emotion, robotic evil is set loose. Similarly, reactive outbursts, arguments, physical violence, and other social evils result when emotion is unmoored from the intellect. Thus, the two must be integrated for the human organism to be balanced and actively human. Imbalance is yet another deviation from the original plan set forth by Olodumare.

Okanran's metaphor is of one who humbly beats floormats, cleaning them of dirt. This precision in describing the trait of humility is breathtaking. When we think of the one who beats the mat to loosen embedded dirt, we think of humility—the performance of unseen and undervalued actions toward the well-being of the mat-beater and others.

The mat-beater benefits as richly as those who use the mat. And so, at the base of humility is a constructive self-interest. Life is just happier sitting on a well-beaten mat. The mat-beater is as comfortable as the others sitting on the mat. In truth, what is being beaten is the ego, as constructive self-interest includes others in the beneficial outfall.

Okanran stands as the solution to the out-of-proportion ego drive. While the ego looks out at the world and sees it as its oyster, humility does the same and realizes it's part of a greater whole. Humility does not presume primacy, whereas ego demands it at the expense of others.

When the follower of Ifá is led to the realization that the ego is standing in the way of spiritual development, Okanran instigates the cycle that provokes it. The ego must be contained for humility to rush into the space the ego formerly had "hogged."

The negative aspect of Okanran results from failing to balance emotions with thoughts. The first line of attack is balancing thoughts and emotions, strengthening the Ori, and growing humility to its rightful stature.

When humility is grown, life is renewed. We arrive at the understanding that our subjective reading of the world around us, placing ourselves at its center, is delusional. Here, we truly confront reality, looking into its depths to discover the truth: That we are part of something much larger than us or our restless egos. The next cycle of life is freshly realized as humility slides into its seat and begins to grow its influence.

Iwa Pele

Good character is rooted in humility, and in Ifá, a good (or gentle) character is called "Iwa Pele." Throughout the Odù, Ifá is referenced, guiding to achieving Iwa Pele. As you have seen, this guidance is summarized in the Sixteen Commandments, making clear what one of good character does and does not do.

Iwa Pele seeks humility but also generosity, wisdom, truth, and patience. Good character is rooted in humility because humility understands that it needs to grow to fill the character of the human it is seeded in. That growth feeds the quest for the other virtues Iwa Pele thirsts after to nourish itself as a spirit prepared for life.

However, the cultivation of Iwa Pele is also for the sake of the community central to the practice of Ifá. A community characterized by all these virtues is happy and mindful of others and spirit. Such a community attracts the favor of the ancestors, Orisha and Olodumare.

When these gentle virtues are practiced, the community learns the meaning of peace, preparing the way of the Iwa Pele to the life of the spirit, informed, and sanctified by Odù Ifá. And community is the model of Faith. Creating human communities of Iwa Pele and restoring community between both halves of the cosmic gourd paves the way for eternally revolving cycles of transformative change.

Humility in Ifá means something more than it means to most of us. Ifá's vision of humility encompasses the understanding that we are not islands and do not succeed because of our inimitable personal virtue. We succeed as part of a community of actors participating as one to create that success.

Yet, something the West will not understand is that Ifá does not strictly adhere to the concept of an individualized soul. In Ifá, while Ori is assigned to the individual, it is but an emanation of Olodumare, the essence of the Divine in our mortal bodies and Ori. Humility, in Ifá, is the setting of the human ego within a great whole of which she is neither better nor worse, lesser, or greater. Ifá teaches that all is one thing, emanating from the same Divine source. In that model, humility is the conduit by which humanity might again reflect the Divine intention for it.

Okanran is about knowing our place in the grand cosmology of things, not pretending we have any special rights exceeding or challenging those of others. The mat-beater's humility is toward the benefit of the whole, ensuring it does its part for the integrity of all in Olodumare.

Ifá Will Mend It

"It will not be spoiled in our own time.
It will not be spoiled in our own time.
The world will not be spoiled in our own time.
Ifá will mend it."

Wande Abimbola

Ògúnwáñdé "Wande" Abímbólá is a Nigerian academician and professor of Yoruba language and literature. He is also a Chief, installed by the Babalawos of Yorubaland, and his definition of Ifá is that of a salvific philosophy of living that is Divinely mandated.

Wande Abimbola teaches language and literature in Nigeria.
https://unsplash.com/photos/wiUl_NyafcY

"Ifá will mend it" is a strong and unequivocal statement, and again, the daily righteousness of Haredi Jews comes to mind, with their assertion that the practice of the 613 mitzvot will restore

Creation. The implication in Ifá is the same, stating that by practicing the Sixteen Commandments and following the teachings offered in divination, the grand project of restoring the integrity of the cosmos will be achieved.

While many religions feature cleansing destruction, positing that Creation will rise from its ashes, Ifá chooses the "home improvements" method. Instead of tearing the whole thing down, it seeks to mend the structure, restoring it to its original condition.

In Judaism, this means the practice of ethically driven, humble living, unmoved by the promptings of the restless human ego. However, this humble living is not intended as a sacrifice or cage in Ifá. Living in a community and in mindfulness of that community's well-being is a template for a satisfying life on earth. The practice of Ifá benefits every living human and all Creation. It is the practice of living in the moment for the future and the past because past, present, and future are all one thing held within a now that determines the health of the integrated whole. In this model, the now is the pivot point.

That pivot point is most dynamic in the practice of divination. As discussed, divination is a guide, allowing supplicants seeking the support of the Babalawo/Iyalawo to impact the progress of their destinies by following the advice of the Odù indicated and the priest's interpretations of it. This agency on the part of the followers of Ifá is the exercise of free will within a communal framework. Within that framework, the individual seeks the most beneficial action for their and the community's well-being.

The now, in Ifá, is part of the eternal revolution of time, with past, present, and future interacting in mysterious ways that result in destinies realized. "Ifá will mend it," as Chief Wande wrote, is a statement set in the future. Like an affirmation, it's a confident statement of a future reality. Ifá has been mending the world for 8,000 years. It's mending the world now. It will mend the world tomorrow. Chief Wande's statement rejects the eschatology of other religions, placing the world's fate firmly in the hands of the living and the religion they follow.

The archetype of humility, Okanran, is a thematic pillar of Ifá, linking all its complex themes back to a single quality. The mending of the world depends on humility, and Ifá acts not as a private club for those who practice a religion to soothe their souls. Ifá acts as a gift to the world, the actions of the faithful mending what has become obsolete or damaged. Nothing in Creation is beyond repair. It's only in need of the love of communal action, directed to the healing of Creation.

The negative manifestation of Obara (strength/ego) is conquered by the ascension of the mat-beating Okanran, as dust is removed so that all might again enjoy the mat in humility. As Chief Wande has written, Ifá will mend it.

In the next chapter, we move on to the Odù Ifá III.

Chapter Ten: Odù Ifá III, Part One — Ogunda and Osa

In this chapter, we will examine Ogunda and Osa, the first two Odù s of Odù Ifá III. The theme of transformative change is central to this chapter, with Ogunda and Osa serving that project in their respective and complementary functions. (NB: The themes are the same as those found in Chapter Six, with Ogbe and Oyeku, with the energies expressed in the respective Odu personified somewhat differently. It is interesting to note that distinctions like these are part of the didactic process of Ifá divination.)

Ogunda

Ogunda is an archetype of transformation, but in that archetype is the ability to remove obstacles. What is created by this natural energy is the creation of opportunity and the enabling of new cycles of growth and personal development.

Many of the obstacles Ogunda removes are self-imposed. Human beings and the egos we struggle with can lead us into all kinds of behaviors damaging to ourselves, our communities, and our destinies.

Most religions speak of intemperate behavior as detrimental to the human soul. Ifá discusses this behavior as preventing the Ori from operating as intended to and interfering with and corroding the community's well-being. Overindulgence in alcohol, drug use, fighting, and other bad human habits has a distinct ripple effect recognized in this communally focused Faith.

Ogunda speaks directly to the practitioner's connection to the Ori and all the things that stand in the way of that crucial connection. Ego is one of the great obstacles—especially to the growth of humility (as discussed in the last chapter). When permitted to explode to the degree at which the self is the pre-eminent, ego leads to aberrant behaviors that are disruptive and damaging to the self and others.

Ogunda's role in transformation is to clear away the obstacles that prevent us from moving through eternity unimpeded by negative habits of thought and emotion. In the integrated Ori, the seat of destiny is cleansed of roadblocks and debris, allowing the free movement of the intellect, emotions, and spirit toward destiny.

Patience and Self-Control

Chief among the attributes taught by Odù Ogunda are patience and self-control. Patience is a function of the balanced individual. Emotion is tempered by thought, and thought is filtered through emotion. Considered are not only the emotions of the person seeking out Ogunda but also those of others, in the family and community. When patience is fostered in the self, perspective is reached, and the ability to see clearly without bias or self-deception is achieved.

Self-control is a tremendous problem for many people. We do not think before we act, and we don't question the validity of our thoughts. In the heat of the moment, we rarely take a moment to interrogate where our thoughts are leading us. However, to be humble, we must. Humility is the breath we take before white-hot rage spills out from the mouth, burning all it touches.

Ogunda is a proving ground for the human's command of Ori. To honor and live in the trajectory of our true destiny, our egotistical self-indulgence and self-obsession must be subjected to the backhoe of Ogunda. If it is not serving your destiny, it's getting leveled.

Self-control is not biting the tongue; self-control is a level-headed self-examination that does not start seconds before a potential interpersonal conflict. The ability to control emotions and meet discord with equanimity and placid confidence is an everyday discipline practiced for a lifetime. It gets easier, but because we are human, the work is never done.

Back to Iwa Pele

As you learned in the last chapter, Iwa Pele is a good or gentle character. This is another pillar of Ifá. A person of good character is alive to the Ori, and their destiny is born within her.

A person of gentle character can also better control their emotions and is endlessly patient with the curveballs of life and the people who throw them. This person understands that everything changes and evolves and that the fewer roadblocks there are to impede evolutionary change, the better off Creation will eventually be. Ifá will mend it.

In Ogunda is the training of the character. Turning the human tendency to overindulge in bad habits toward the nobler pursuit of following and realizing Ori is the fruit of Ogunda, the remover of obstacles and the creator of opportunities and new horizons.

Fundamental to Iwa Pele is the temperament because it is in the temperament that we see the truth about people. We see their maturity or lack thereof in their ability to control emotional reactions. In the human temperament are the makings of leadership.

As you are reading, hopefully, you're connecting with the interplay of the energies represented by the Odùs that we are discussing. As you can see, what is emerging is a snapshot of the Odù Ifá's mission: To teach followers the lessons learned by the ancestors and collected by the Babalawo/Iyalawo as templates for living. Every Odù has a specific energy, discussing similar and overlapping themes. Within each energy is the vibration of every variation and what it means in terms of living with integrity in the Ifá model. And all this is to transform the follower's life to be in line with the purpose of destiny, both collective and individual. In each Odùs is a world of self-development and information about how we might better ourselves for the good of all.

Iwa Pele is the goal of all Ifá followers. In Ogunda, the patience and self-control needed to achieve the status of Iwa Pele are nurtured by clearing away what's impeding progress. That brings us to Osa, which is another clearing away with explosive implications.

Osa

All that occurs in life cannot be traced to our own actions. Saying that is true is repeating fiction. Reality precludes the fantastical belief that we control it. We control our reactions to what happens but do not control reality. We are the subjects of reality, and we choose how we respond to that subject status. That is our locus of control—our response.

Osa is the stuff we have no control over. It is a riverbank breaking, forcing water into the street, pushing vehicles with its fearsome strength. Osa is the thunderstorm, the chunks of hail that dent the roofs of cars. Osa is an earthquake that levels a town. Osa is the unexpected, the catastrophic.

However, in cataclysm, there is the shock of rebirth. When all has been suddenly torn down, there is no choice but to build back up, which is one of the tenets of Ifá. All that has been made is subject to change. Nothing is complete. Nothing is perfect. Change does not stop. In the ever-evolving cosmos of Ifá, what is no longer serving its purpose is transformed, recycled, and reused. It's restored to more closely reflect the Divine Will's original intention.

Cataclysm as Revolution

Osa, as mentioned above, is the unexpected cataclysm. Just when you think all your ducks are in a tidy row, along comes Osa to disavow your silly assumptions. In our comfort and self-congratulation for how great our lives our, we forget that anything can happen. We forget that our presumed virtue is not a bulwark against the unpredictable.

Major illness may be more in the realm of Oronwin, who is the chaos serving order. While unexpected, it comes from within. It comes from our destiny, and how we choose to confront a major illness is where the learning takes place. On the other hand, Osa is entirely external to us, crashing into our well-ordered lives like a rampaging bull.

Anything can happen in a natural world increasingly being challenged by human activity, giving rise to extreme weather of all kinds. The natural world is rebelling, dealing out punishing hurricanes to destructive tsunamis, and we are part of that world. Intrinsic to, yet in awe of it, we find ourselves in the path of the natural world's rebellion against us.

And when it hits us, the world we know that feeds us, waters us, and is our home is suddenly an enemy, threatening to remove us from its surface. The standard response is "Why?" "Why me?" "Why here?" There is nothing we can do. We either pack up and get out of the path of whatever natural disaster is bearing down on us, or we stay, taking our chances. The latter option was taken by many in New Orleans, Los Angeles, as Hurricane Katrina bore down on Crescent City on August 29, 2005. New Orleans residents had been through it all before. Many hurricanes had buffeted the city over its long life and reside in the recent memory of residents. Some New Orleanians felt that they knew the drill and had the lay of the land. They had their ducks in a row, and so, they stayed.

Many died. Many lost homes that had been in their families for generations. But almost two decades after the Federal Levee Disaster of New Orleans—a clue as to how chaos only serves order it recognizes as order—New Orleanians continue to sing:

> "*Meanwhile, you might as well have a good time.*
>
> *Meanwhile, there may not be the next time.*
>
> *Meanwhile, you better shake that pretty booty, baby.*"
>
> - Ivan Neville, Dumphstahfunk

They continued to live, work and love in New Orleans, knowing that nature could have another go at them. And yet, there they are.

On the Worst Day of Your Life

Everyone holds a narrative about the worst day of their life in their mind. For most New Orleans residents, that was the day the levees broke. It was not enough that a Category 5 hurricane had descended on New Orleans. The levees, constructed by the supposedly competent Army Corps of Engineers, gave way under the onslaught of a powerful hurricane.

Thus, humanity failed to collaborate with nature by limiting its potential for destruction. Nature and its behaviors have no ethics, no morals, no thought. Nature is like the Divine in that respect. Its ways are not our ways. Yet, our ways did not serve the whole of nature on that fateful day by neglecting the human element—the residents of New Orleans.

No one can imagine living such a horrifying day as that day in New Orleans unless they were there. However, one can imagine the terror of all that water coming at them. We have seen the destruction water is capable of, especially when humans neglect to protect those most vulnerable.

Added to the terror of Katrina is the betrayal of other humans of a collective it deemed unworthy of government-funded protection in a hurricane-prone city. How could that day not have been the worst of your life? But Katrina's destruction lasted eight long days, causing almost 2,000 deaths and billions of dollars in damage.

Osa is the cataclysm, while Ogunda holds the key to survival. In the instance of Katrina, the equanimity brings those who survived the courage to go on. After seeing your city swamped, largely abandoned by the federal government, as human bodies floated in the engulfed streets, how do you go on? You just do it because the community is there, and it always will be as long as the land is above water.

As you can see, the energies described in this chapter are synchronous with those discussed in Ogbe and Oyeku in Chapter Six but with divergent energetic agendas. Unexpected change in Oyeku comes from within. In Osa, it is external. Similarly, Ogbe removes obstacles but trusts in service of following the promptings of destiny in the Ori. Ogunda removes obstacles expressed physically in corrosive habits that lead to disunity and dysfunction. The symbols are the same, but the agendas are different in energetic quality.

Meanwhile, back in New Orleans, the city may not have been renewed as hoped, but the culture of the community continues to thrive and grow, springing up from the cataclysm in triumphant joy. Survival is the necessity we must serve in confronting reality, and this is evident in the cultural and communal recovery from Katrina. None of this is attributable to anyone outside that community. All this was and has always been achieved by people who model equanimity as a way of life.

In the lyrics of the song "Meanwhile," shown at the beginning of this chapter, it's not difficult to sense the equanimity of a population accustomed to cataclysm. From Yellow Fever to Katrina, New Orleans has suffered numerous roundhouse kicks. However, through it all, the community has repeatedly risen up in music and culture, ever singing the song of destiny stuck in its throat.

Cyclical Cataclysm and Rebirth

New Orleans is easily identifiable as an icon of Black American culture. With its extraordinary legacy of Second Lines, Mardi Gras Indians, Louis Armstrong, and Little Wayne, the city is a cauldron of Black America's most vibrant links to Africa. Those links are apparent in Voudon, both practiced and celebrated in this majority Roman Catholic city. Hoodoo is also practiced as a living legacy rooted in the abuses of the plantation, some of which still stand in stately splendor to satisfy visitors' curiosity.

Within the cyclical cataclysms that mark New Orleans's long and checkered history are multiple rebirths that speak of an unbreakable spirit. In that spirit are echoes of Ifá. Those echoes are in the patience, fortitude, and equanimity of a people apart, riding the chaos hiding beneath order like a streetcar. They get off at the next stop and join the Second Line parade, picking up the nearest tambourine.

And that is the combined lesson of Ogunda and Osa. With patience and self-control, we get off at the next stop and keep going in full command of our emotions. The past is over. There may not be a next time, but go on and shake that pretty booty because cycles come and go. Life cycles, falling and rising in cataclysmic succession as life leaps riotously from the rubble, which will soon be recycled. Trumpets blow—Tubas throb. The asphalt sings with dancing feet.

This is not to suggest that New Orleans is a microcosm of Ifá practice, but what is clear is that the spirit is there, in the people. No religion can live for 8,000 years and not become part of a people's DNA, both culturally and physically. Visit the Voodoo Temple on Rampart Street and see how true this is. Witness the survival of traditions originating in Haiti (the Second Line and shotgun houses, for starters). Experience people that will not stop dancing, singing, playing, creating, building up, and tearing down as the streets are full to the brim.

Cataclysm and rebirth are the nature of New Orleans, just as they are the nature of Ifá's cosmic gourd. Every catastrophic impact of nature results in its new growth, just as the people know in their souls.

Chapter Eleven: Odù Ifá III, Part Two — Ika and Oturupon

In the second part of our exploration Part III, we explore two Odu/archetypes, which speak to two opposed aspects of the human personality: Power and weakness. We will examine their energetic missions and the interplay between Ika and Oturopon.

Ika

In Ika, the Iwa Pele (good/gentle character) is transformed to become personal power. We all manifest personal power in different ways. In Ika, power is externalized in the invocation of wisdom in the spoken word. Personal power is still the act of affirming the self and its truths, but it is also speaking those truths as a public reflection of the self.

The self cannot be affirmed (entirely) from within. To achieve self-affirmation, a strong sense of self and one's relationship to the world is needed. Most of us, though, will not have such a sense of self until some point in our second decade. Others will not have this sense of self until much later. However, for the most part, we understand ourselves and where we stand in relation to the world and other people by looking at what is reflected by them. From the impressions of others and our interactions with them, we come to learn about ourselves and who we are. We find, as we grow, our power.

But Ika proposes that the person's truth is in the word and the wisdom that drives it. Arising from the Ashé, personal power is the ability to create and participate in change and to make things happen in the world around you.

We have yet to speak of Ashé in this book, but Ika is where Ashé is at its most powerful energetically, leading the believer toward the power within them. In the wisdom-informed word, Ashé is realized, and Ika is where that happens.

Personal power is what holds us all up, giving us the ability to walk down the street, interact with other people, and live our lives. However, personal power is so much more than being able to function in the world. In Ashé, personal power becomes almost material, manifesting as the development of wisdom made whole in the spoken word.

As a sign of power, the spoken word is not surprising from Ifá, a religion that relies on oral tradition to pass down its ancestral wisdom. Wisdom is collected to be shared, and when a written account may not be made, that wisdom must be spoken. In the Babalawo/Iyalawo, the collected wisdom of the ancestors is incarnated as a repository of the sum of Ifá's many gifts. That spoken word is the living voice of the ancestors and the Orisha, speaking as the attributes of a distant God.

Olodumare's Gift

Ashé is the same power that created everything in the universe. It is a direct infusion of the Divine Power into all humans, plants, rocks, water, and everything else. Ashé is the life force that animates and sustains us as creaturely beings. Without Ashé, nothing can exist. It is a Divine gift that lives in all and makes all live.

And Ashé is most powerfully manifested in the spoken word when it speaks in the ancestors' wisdom and acts in that same wisdom. Like the Ori, Ashé is specific to the person, organism, or object it animates. While part of something larger, like Ori, it is contained in its individuality (personal unit of consciousness).

With the gift of divination, Ashé is honored with wisdom, again emphasizing the importance of the practice. As Divine power (potential in the human), Ashé must be fed to become the authoritative voice it is intended to be. With the infusion of wisdom provided by divination, the believer grows in Ashé, reaching its full manifestation in the Ori's destiny.

Ika is where Ashé is grown in the power of the word. As the power of the word is the highest manifestation of Ashé, forming and realizing it is the source of healing and transformation. Ika's negative aspect is the tendency to abuse personal power to indulge in idle gossip at the expense of other people. However, the Ashé, which is well-formed in the wisdom and power of the word, is the true, positive Ashé allowing humanity the luxury of Divine power within a circumscribed theater—the word. From this theater proceeds power infused with wisdom, which brings forward the intentions of Olodumare for Creation's continuing and eternal evolution.

Oturopon

Oturopon is the energy of disease, especially infectious disease. However, it is also the energy of protection against disease. Ika's power is juxtaposed to the weakness inflicted by illness, striking us and laying us low. But the disease is a double-edged sword in the human organism. As we have seen with the pandemic, the immune system can become stronger when exposed to an infectious disease, preventing death and serious, long-term illness.

When COVID arrived, there was no vaccine for it—although science had been attempting to produce one for years. When the vaccine arrived and was disseminated, people were still getting ill from the virus. However, death was routed. These effects increased as second vaccinations and booster shots rolled out. As people's immune systems were strengthened, the virus began to wane, and fewer vulnerable hosts were available to infect; diffusion was radically reduced and is now on the way to being controlled—if not eliminated.

The pandemic taught us some timely lessons about the modern world, its conveniences, speed, and the expectations of people living in it. We learned from the virus that our supply chains are fragile. We learned that while viruses move quickly, science does not. Once a virus has taken hold, eradicating it is a long, painful procedure.

The energy of Oturopon works in precisely the same way. It identifies solutions to illness. But in the energy's negative aspect, the disease is used as a cleansing tool, so Oturopon, like the disease itself, is a double-edged sword. It bears diseases into the world, teaching us how to defend ourselves against them.

And that defense system is the complex of learning available to Ifá believers. When the Ashé is fed by wisdom and expressed in the power of the word, the body is fortified. Because, as mentioned earlier, the mind and body—like everything else that exists—are one thing. There is nobody without the mind, and without the body, what is there for the mind to do? What does it interact with?

Thus, how does the Ori exist? Or the Ashé? How does our power proceed to the next life without the flesh? Simply, the Ori and Ashé are Olodumare in us. Personalized to the individual, yet the raw stuff of Divinity, these aspects of being human in the Ifá model are to be recycled, reused, and reimagined as they move through time. Developed for and by us—and our interactions with the wisdom of the word—the Ori and Ashé are subject to evolution as everything else in the cosmology of this religion is. And because they proceed from Olodumare as gifts, they continue in the service of Olodumare as our cycles turn, and these tiny shards of destiny and personal power continue to their next adventure. As they do, their learning continues, feeding Creation with the distant God's now recycled, eternal gifts.

The framing of destiny and power as gifts of God, bestowed and thus intended to serve God, frees them to proceed into eternity. In each cycle of its material existence, the body has transformed with the mind to accomplish the simultaneous unfolding of destiny. It is not obsolete, so much as needed to feed the earth as the Ori and Ashé proceed on their eternal journey.

Self-Defense Is the Power of the Word

Oturopon both bears to us and cures us of disease. Infectious physical diseases are just the start because the greatest diseases humanity is prone to are diseases of the mind: Vanity, rage, deceit, self-obsession, and hatred are only some of them. In the power of the word, these diseases are dispatched from the mind. However, our spiritual and intellectual immune systems are strengthened as they are. The Ashé grows in the human organism unencumbered by disease. When Ashé is strong, the body is strong because the mind is strong.

By creating disease and proposing the solution to feeding the Ashé, Oturopon confronts us with reality. We are creatures of Olodumare, and as creatures, we are well-served by the practice of divination, in which we discover our personal power—the ultimate defense against the ills that human life falls prey to. The power of a human being reinforced with the ancestors' wisdom is difficult to breach. It is also exemplary, presenting the community with the power of the word infused with wisdom.

Ika and Oturopon have a dynamic message about the nature of being human holistically and mindfully. The threats we fear are the threats we must prepare ourselves for every day of our lives. They are neither distant nor near. These threats are a potential awaiting opportunity. We defend ourselves against them through the practice of accumulating and acting upon wisdom to the benefit of mind and body as one integrated reality.

Defending against threats to the organism's health is a function of divination, which has the power to shift destiny. Ika defends, while Oturopon reminds believers why defense is an imperative. The wisdom of the powerful, word-infused Aché, reflecting Olodumare, reflects the ancestors' wisdom serving that God. This is the raw, Divine power that created all. In the human organism, it can serve, or it can flounder. In service, it stands as an imago dei (image of the Divine), showing forth the strength of generations of wisdom that pervades every cell and structure of the follower whose personal power is rooted in the word.

In divination, the supplicant's life is connected to the life of the ancestors and the spirit world. With the mediating word of Odù

Ifá reaching across time—and across the two halves of the cosmic gourd—a cure to the diseases of humanity is found. The true Aché's power is reinforced, and the supplicant is freed to live in the intended destiny of the Ori.

The word that reaches out to humanity in divination for the ordering of life and the realization of destiny contains the healing humans seek. Every level of healing is evident here, in body/mind, in community, and between humans and the spirit world. Ika's call to develop personal power in the word is intrinsic to this oral tradition. The oral tradition at the center of Ifá is encapsulated in this demand for power to be lived out in the word of wisdom as the expression of Aché that is most attuned to its source—Olodumare.

Next, we move on to the last part of Odù Ifá covered in this book. While we are only skimming the surface here and providing information for the sake of interest, hopefully, you continue seeking. The Ifá Faith, as you have seen, is complex and sophisticated. It is worth a much deeper exploration than the one offered in these pages.

Chapter Twelve: Odù Ifá IV — Otura, Irete, Ose, and Ofun

Our final chapter about the Odù Ifá contains the four Odu of Part IV. As explained at the start of Chapter Six, these four Odu are less complex—especially after absorbing many valuable narratives from the Odù Ifá in previous chapters.

Otura

In the world of Otura, comfort is the ability to view everything through the lens of mysticism. This unique type of vision represents the follower finding their way to Olodumare by sharing in the Divine vision.

The root of mysticism is the Ori, and the foundation of the Ori, fully integrated and groomed for eternity, is Otura. Otura is the follower's purpose and destiny. When these are aligned with those of Olodumare, the follower of Ifá is in sync with their intended purpose.

The negative side of Otura is directing the Ori toward the wrong identification, which usually manifests as extreme identification with a group outside the framework of Ifá. Nationalism, racism, and narcissistic self-obsession (extreme identification with the self above all) are examples of mistaken and corrosive identification in Otura.

Mysticism is the comfort of belonging to something immaterial. It is the embrace of the supernatural world, guiding the individual toward the unseen, as a mother hen guides its chicks to the coop.

Derived from the Greek word *mysterion*, meaning "secret ritual or belief," this word is a derivative of the Greek *mystes*, meaning "novice." The root of *mystes* is *muen*, which means to "close" (referring to the mouth/eyes). The implication is that mysticism is a process that is both internal and independent of the physical senses. Mysticism is not pursued by discussions or seeing, or learning; mysticism is experienced at the core of the human being who aligns with the Holy Source.

Mysticism seeks a fundamental connection of the human being to the Source of all that is. Part of that connection is its personal, intimate nature, creating a very specific variety of embraces shared between the human mystic and the Divine Source. This connection is union, and the union is the nature of the Ifá religion, advancing the notion that everything residing in either half of the cosmic gourd resides in the unity of purpose and spirit.

Irete

Irete is like a winepress. From life, it presses the stroke of luck; we all need to have successful lives. However, there is more to Irete than the provision of good fortune. Irete is about determination because determination is what it takes to arrive at the abundance we all desire in life. Determination is required to transform oneself according to the urgings of the Ori and the work of divination. Comforted by the mysticism of Otura, the follower can discern the way forward and leverage determination with the support of divination, guiding and leading with the wisdom of the Odù Ifá.

Irete is bullheaded, demanding that the follower of Ifá hang on to the destiny they have been given and grow it into reality. However, that bullheaded determination can have a negative flip side. That same quality can be misdirected, leading the follower astray with goals that are not tied to their destiny. Worse still, that stubbornness can be negatively transformed into a refusal to change and improve.

Stubbornness has a negative reputation, but it has a purpose. That purpose is not to be stuck in a self stunted by a bullheaded refusal to move forward, change, and grow to come to the full stature of what it means to be a human being practicing Ifá. Irete's purpose is to birth in the follower of Ifá the stubbornness to not give up on themselves or on Olodumare and the Orisha, who represent the distant God.

With the mysticism of Otura influencing the follower, Irete grows into the kind of stubbornness that realizes earthly dreams and builds the Ori for its journey through eternity and its purpose. The two are intimately connected, with mysticism guiding the believer toward their destiny in the spirit world and Irete guiding the believer on earth because on earth, as material beings, we create the template of the Ori's eternity, improving the lives of those around us and growing to be the example others follow.

Ose

The Odu/archetype of Ose is primarily concerned with creating abundance. While Irete teaches and guides the follower to be steadfast in their pursuit of abundance, Ose's underpinnings are in the world and its power. It goes further than Ika (Chapter Eleven) in that it specifically refers to prayer and the use of the word as its basis.

Ose also refers to reproduction and the realization of Irosun (menstrual blood and the womb). Children, in Ifá, are a manifestation of abundance and the materialization of the promise of Irosun. While Irosun refers to all abundance, Ose is more specific in its intentions, directly confronting followers with the imperative to be "fruitful and multiply."

In the world of Ose, abundance and fertility are in the word itself, expressed in prayer. And human sexuality is, naturally, a huge part of that process. The erotic is celebrated and uplifted in Ose, taking pride of place as a key source of human abundance. However, this is not the eroticism of the sex-addled West; this is the eroticism of the desire for children, the erotic playing a key part in the gift of reproduction. Desire is at the heart of Ose, but it is a desire that sees its ultimate end in procreative abundance.

Without humanity's erotic desire, Ose is mocked, and children are not produced, and so, the erotic is canonized in the practice of Ifá in this Odu/archetype. United with Otura's soul-comforting, Ori-growing mysticism, and Irete's squeezing out of life's goodness, Ose conquers by creating abundance that speaks of the family's success, the couple's ardor, and love for one another, and the loving unity of the distant God's Creation.

Lastly, the power of the word is like the abundance of water, causing new life to spring forth. When poured out in prayer, Ose pours abundance on the people. The wisdom-informed word becomes the source of abundance as a manifestation of Olodumare's will, delivering the blessings always intended for humanity, including progeny.

Ofun

Ofun is light. This is the light by which the material world is seen and experienced. Everything you see is seen under the light of Ofun. That is not to say that Ofun is analogous, energetically, to Olodumare. Ofun is an Odu/archetype, energetically acting on the will of Olodumare.

This Odu/archetype is the light of the material world, causing miracles to occur but only by the power of the word. Ika and Ose conspire in Ofun to shine a light on what's stagnant—in need of transformation and regeneration. When the wisdom-informed word is spoken, Ofun reveals the light in the form of miracles.

Answered prayer is Ofun's work in creation, fleshing the power of the word with a response. That response may not be the miracle we envisioned, but it is a miracle. It's in keeping up with destiny, giving us what we needed but which we might not have asked for. We might not have asked for anything, yet the miraculous touches us.

In Ofun, the word's power is ignited, creating a two-way communicative dynamic. The believer calls out to Creation with the word, and Ofun shines the light that reveals the miracle, creating something new.

Interplay and Realization

This final chapter is not unlike a summation of the Principle Odus of Odù Ifá. These four Odu represent the interplay and realization of all the preceding Odu, encompassing the promise of divination for supplicants who come to the priest for guidance and wisdom.

Otura's mysticism pierces the believer, tethering them to the spirit world. Mysticism's leading hand is unseen, immaterial, and known only to the believer. This direct experience of the Divine is unavailable as a shared experience. It exists only in the believer's heart, experiencing God as God is. From this profound place of communion, Irete is born, bringing forth the goodness of the Created Order through the bullheaded determination of the believer. Abundance results but as a gift of the believer to God. It is the efforts of the believer that create abundance. The abundance of Irete is not just a gift; it results from unity with all that is and the actions that proceed due to that unity. Those actions are steadfast and dedicated, never wavering from their objectives. In Ose, the power of the word is the font of procreation and the eroticism which leads to it, realizing the promise of Irosun's womb and menstrual blood. Children are Ose's version of abundance and the manifestation of Irosun. Ofun sheds light on Creation's true form, resulting in miracles as the answer to the wisdom-infused word in prayer.

These four Odu speak to the entire deposit of ancestral knowledge represented by the Odù Ifá as the refined sum of the principal Odu we have read. Every parable, narrative, and poem included in this collection of life lessons hinges on the contents of the sixteen Odu.

The themes of abundance, procreation, and miracles in response to prayer stand as a capsule version of what life is intended to be like in the Ifá cosmology. When humanity has been rightly ordered by orthopraxis, the legacy of that ordering is wrapped in mysticism that leads to abundance. Embodied by the human voice invoking the word in prayer, the light of Ofun pours out on Creation the miracles possible for humanity aligned with the original vision of Olodumare.

The work of eternity is performed when you live, think, and act as a co-creative element in Creation. The cosmic gourd's two halves draw closer together, and God is near again. While Olodumare may not be "just down the block," God is no longer quite so distant, as humanity keeps its part of the bargain.

The Fruit

In these four, Odu is the form of the divine plan for humanity, laid out as a challenge. Humanity has the power to realize the dream of Olodumare: That the cosmic gourd is again whole as one thing, undivided by the grossness of humanity's cavalier behavior.

In learning not to toss our apple cores on God's lawn, we rise to the intended stature of the forms first breathed into by Olodumare as fashioned by Obatala. That dream is one of unity and right action, flowing from the lessons learned in divination, the core of Ifá practice and life. In the Odù Ifá, the guiding lessons and tales of the ancestors draw humanity a picture: This is how human beings should be; this is how they think and behave because this is how the ancestors responded to the challenges and opportunities of life.

The practicality of Ifá is a framework for its mysticism and the promise of an eternity spent recycling, renewing, and reusing the stuff of Creation, just as Olodumare did at the Creative Moment. From the swampy land, Obatala created better earth. It was not a trick with mirrors but a construction project that built a better Creation from existing matter. Today, that project continues in the work of the people of Olodumare, the Ifá, in a religious lifestyle and philosophy of life intended to benefit not just themselves but every living thing.

Without beginning or end, time moves in a circle lived out in human life and the spirit world as a continual and persistent revolution. Refining and bending, pressing and praying, learning, and teaching, the people of Ifá, live their co-creative role in the world as a lifestyle that has persisted for 8,000 years. The next 8,000 years and the years following are not promised, but the Ifá know that time's cycles are set to revolve. And revolve they will, eternally and without cessation.

Conclusion

Your journey into the heart of one of the world's oldest and most sophisticated religions is just starting. Hopefully, this book left you wanting to learn more about Ifá and has encouraged you to continue exploring this ancient religious system and its message to humanity. That message is yours to formulate for yourself. However, at its core, it is a message of working with God to form and reform Creation until it aligns with the vision of Olodumare.

Human beings are given a lofty goal in Ifá, building with the Great Architect the best version of themselves to build one of the best versions of Creation possible. Imagine what a difference that thought might make to the world if we were all to take it to heart.

May your journey continue, and may you know peace and harmony in this life and those that follow.

Here's another book by Mari Silva that you might like

YORUBA

THE ULTIMATE GUIDE TO IFA
SPIRITUALITY, ISESE, ODU,
ORISHAS, SANTERIA, AND MORE

MARI SILVA

Your Free Gift (only available for a limited time)

Thanks for getting this book! If you want to learn more about various spirituality topics, then join Mari Silva's community and get a free guided meditation MP3 for awakening your third eye. This guided meditation mp3 is designed to open and strengthen ones third eye so you can experience a higher state of consciousness. Simply visit the link below the image to get started.

https://spiritualityspot.com/meditation

Bibliography

AfrikaIsWoke.Com. *Ifa oracle: The 16 Odu Ifa & their meaning.* (2022, February 3). https://www.afrikaiswoke.com/ifa-oracle-the-16-odu-ifa-their-meaning/

Atlanta University Center Woodruff Library. (2022). *African traditional religions: Ifa.* Atla. https://atla.libguides.com/c.php?g=1138564&p=8386152

Bascom, W. R. (1969). *Ifa divination: Communication between gods and men in West Africa.* Indiana University Press.

Dev, B. (2016, February 4). *Eight interesting facts about the Yoruba people.* Bashiri. https://bashiri.com.au/eight-interesting-facts-yoruba-people/

Faseyin, A. Z., & Faseyin, F. A. Y. (2006). *IWAKERI: The quest for Afrikan spirituality by Awotunde Yao Zannu Faseyin.* Lulu Enterprises Incorporated.

Harvard University. (n.d.). *Ifa.* https://projects.iq.harvard.edu/predictionx/ifa

Odutola, K. (2019. *Yoruba culture & customs.* Ufl.Edu.

Packer, M. J., & Tibaduiza Sierra, S. (2012). A concrete psychological investigation of ifá divination. *Revista Colombiana de Psicología, 21*(2), 355–371.

Study.Com. *Yoruba people: Language, culture & music.* (n.d.). https://study.com/academy/lesson/yoruba-people-language-culture-music.html

Walker, R. A. (2009). *The arts of Africa at the Dallas Museum of Art.* Yale University Press.

Winn, L. M., & Jacknis, I. (Eds.). (2004.). *Yoruba art & culture.* University of California. https://hearstmuseum.berkeley.edu/wp-content/uploads/TeachingKit_YorubaArtAndCulture.pdf

Printed in the USA
CPSIA information can be obtained
at www.ICGtesting.com
LVHW021059231023
761842LV00001B/1